Please remember that this is a library book, and that it belongs only temporarily to each person who uses it. Be considerate. Do not write in this, or any, library book.

WHAT'S COLLEGE FOR?

vc- m.Ed

WHAT'S COLLEGE FOR?

The Struggle to Define American Higher Education

ZACHARY KARABELL

BASIC
BOOKS

A Member of the Perseus Books Group

Published by Basic Books,
A Member of the Perseus Books Group

Designed by Rachel Hegarty

Library of Congress Cataloging-in-Publication Data
Karabell, Zachary.
    What's college for? : the struggle to define American higher
education / Zachary Karabell.
        p.   cm.
    Includes bibliographical references (p.   ) and index.
    ISBN 0-465-09152-0
    1. Education, Higher—Aims and objectives—United States.
    2. Education, Higher—Social aspects—United States.   3. Education,
Humanistic—United States.   4. College students—United States—
Attitudes.   5. Teacher-student relationships—United States.
    I. Title.
    LA227.4.K37   1998
    378.73--dc21   98-30874
                                                                 CIP

98 99 00 01 ❖ / RRD 10 9 8 7 6 5 4 3 2 1

CONTENTS

INTRODUCTION

There was a time when the question "What's college for?" would have elicited an answer extolling the value of education as a necessary step up the social ladder. Parents dispatched their sons to college, and on occasion daughters, for that slip of paper that proclaimed the graduate acceptable to any corporation or profession, trained to handle himself through a long lifetime of trying social situations. If pressed, college-bound students and their parents would certainly admit to a financial consideration as well. That same slip of paper that certified the college graduate as interesting salon company also helped open career doors otherwise closed to those not high born. But even here the advantage of a college experience came from the reality that business was conducted among gentlemen who preferred the company of others with an appreciation of those finer things in life—art, music, literature, history, and philosophy.

Today, the "value of an education" is calculated in a more straightforward way: in terms of lifetime dollars and cents potentially to be earned. Indeed, working- and middle-class parents are now regularly spending or borrowing $50,000 to $100,000 per child to give their children the benefits of a college education because they know that without the degree their child's life chances will be severely restricted. And there is little disagreement on this point. That college is the single most important factor in getting launched in a career is no longer challenged by anyone, at least not in the U.S. But what is starting to open up as a question ready for debate is where the benefit comes from: Are college-educated children better able to compete for jobs and have successful careers because of the translatable skills they acquire in the process of learning sociology, or history, or gender studies? Or is it just a case of credentials? A candidate with the proper degree is so strongly presumed to be better able to the do the job that it makes no sense for the person doing the hiring to risk offering the opening to a candidate without it.

In asking questions about what a college education should give a student in addition to the degree, students and parents are responding to a recent but very real concern. At the close of the twentieth century, possessing a diploma is not necessarily enough to guarantee one either a good job or even any job. As business is now organized, most jobs are not lifelong, and career changes occur frequently. And here, it is skills rather than credentials, even the skill to be able to learn what needs to be learned to shift careers midway through life, that seem more influential in determining who best weathers career crises.

As students come to realize that they had better come out of college with more than a piece of paper certifying them as educated, but with skills that truly make them more productive workers or more imaginative entrepreneurs, the question of what people are learning in college will be getting much more attention.

Who determines what students learn? Everyone knows the answer to that one. Professors. And the word is *professors* and not *teachers* because although the two words are used almost interchangeably, professors do not see themselves as teachers. At least not by mission. A teacher is someone whose professional goal is helping students learn. Professors are people trained to do cutting-edge research. They teach for several purposes: In exchange for teaching, they get a salary, an institutional setting, and an opportunity to do their research, and they get to expose students to that research.

This system creates few problems for undergraduates in the elite colleges, many of whom will indeed go on to become the next generation of professors at all levels of higher education. But such students represent a very small part of the college population. The student at Podunk U. who is working part time as well as taking out government loans has neither the time nor the desire to be exposed to the newest trends in historical or literary analysis. While those trends are the lifeblood of academic fields, the student who will never work in academia gets little value from exposure to those debates.

Meanwhile, the president of the United States announces that at least two years of college should be every American's right, not select Americans' privilege. Congress passes a generous $40-billion package of tax breaks and scholarships with minimal public discussion and comparatively little partisan debate.[1] In light of the problems of secondary education, college has now become the socializing mechanism of choice for parents and politicos. Students, taking the cue, flock to schools in record numbers.

And for what? Each day, in thousands of classrooms around the country, professors and students stare at each other not comprehending the wide gulf that exists between them. Professors don't simply privilege research; they have neither the training nor the inclination to be teachers to students who graduate high school without many basic skills. Many of these professors are also severely underpaid and hired part-time for as little as $1,500 a term.[2] This split between what professors are trained to do and what public institutions of higher learning hire them to do affects every professor, every student, and by extension, the society as a whole. If each doctor in this country were trained to expect a life of intense research, then we would have tens of thousands of doctors at local clinics ill suited to the demands of public health. Yet, that's precisely the problem in universities, with tens of thousands of professors not attuned to the public good of higher education. This raises troubling questions about the large sums being spent and the vast amount of energy and time that the average American now spends trying to obtain a college degree.

As the United States enters the twenty-first century, a quiet revolution is occurring: Higher education is becoming mass education and in the process is being radically democratized. Almost two-thirds of high school graduates now go to college. We spend more than $175 billion on higher education each year, nearly as much as we spend on defense and almost twenty times what we spend on Hollywood movies. One hundred and nine billion dollars of the total was spent on public institutions, and state legislatures ponied up more than $44 billion of that amount. There are now almost 16 million students, 13 million of them undergraduates. Fifty-five percent of them are women, many of them attending part-time, and many of them "mature " students in their thirties and forties. In 1995, there were 3,688 public and private colleges and universities in the United States, and since 1960, enrollment at public two-year colleges has increased from less than five hundred thousand to nearly 6 million. In the past two decades, the face of higher education has been altered dramatically and irrevocably.[3] Now, and even more in the future, what goes on in the university is inseparable from who we are as a nation.

Therefore, the struggles between students and professors, between professors and other professors, and between the larger society and the culture of academia have consequences for us all. It is not in any of our interests for any one group to win. Students should not be able to dictate how they are graded; state legislatures should not be the sole deciders of how much we spend; and professors should not be the only arbiters of what they teach, how they spend their time, and what they study. But while no one group should define the purpose of college, the various parties need a far more complex and subtle understanding of each other.

This book calls on everyone involved in higher education to consider what college is for. At present, that is not happening. While the university and its function in educating Americans are undergoing such a fundamental transformation, the public discussion on higher education is still dominated by angry conservatives and equally angry voices on the left arguing about the state of knowledge in general and the humanities in particular.[4] But both sides have been so busy hurling invective at one another that they haven't noticed that the real battles are elsewhere. The most pressing issue in higher education today is the widening chasm between professors and the larger society. That chasm isn't the function of ideology; it's a by-product of the culture of academia, a culture that in fundamental ways hasn't changed in decades even as the world around undergoes radical transformations. The culture of academia and its professional structures may not lend themselves to hyperbolic rhetoric; they may not be as easy to reduce to soundbites; but they are the source of most tensions in higher education today.

I have spent much of my adult life as either a teacher or a student. I have sat in classrooms listening to brilliant professors wanting the discussion to continue after the hour came to an end. I have also slumped in my seat trying desperately to stay awake. I have been astounded at the skill and dedication of some professors, and dismayed at the mediocrity of others. As a graduate student, I was mentored by some of academia's best and brightest, and they did their best to guide me toward a career as a scholar. And as a teacher at the University of Massachusetts, Harvard, and Dartmouth, I have taught history to hundreds of students, some engaged and interested, others just warming their seats. I have attended dozens of academic conferences and talked with other professors and high school teachers. This book is the product of these experiences.

In addition, I have visited dozens of campuses and talked with hundreds of students and professors. While a handful of them are still locked in a debate over the curriculum and the "great books," the overwhelming majority have different concerns, and most classes focus on worries more mundane and immediate than the arcane debate between conservative cultural critics and radical academics. Those combatants have set the parameters of the cultural debate. But at best, they focus on the extremes, on the doctrinaire Afrocentric professor, the relativist Western civilization course, the need for an explicit canon, a "cultural literacy." What about the experience of teachers and students in the college classroom? What is happening on the front line? What is happening not in the extreme Afrocentrist course, but in a moderate department of a second-tier university? Is it really as simple as an abandonment of elitism, as the late William Henry said? Is there a decline in moral virtue, in a belief in standards, as William Bennett suggests? Is a war against traditional, white male culture really being waged by academics in the classroom?

The answer to these questions is no. Oh, it's easy enough to find egregious examples of professors abandoning standards, advocating one narrow-minded ideology or another, and trying to subvert "traditional" values. But these are the exceptions, not the norm. A vast terrain is left unexamined by the culture-wars debate. The changes in higher education, in the types of students, the lives of graduate students, and the careers of professors, these issues are all but invisible in public discourse, yet they matter far more to most people in the university today than which translation of Plato is used. In the midst of the fray between cultural critics and "tenured radicals," newly minted Ph.D.'s are caught between the demands of their guild to publish articles and books that reflect the narrow sensibilities of the current body of tenured professors and the demands of their students to learn histories that speak to their experience.

The real frontline struggle in higher education is not within the groves of elite academe. At places like Harvard and Wellesley, Princeton and Georgetown, there is a deceptive calm. Everything looks much the same as it did twenty or thirty years ago. The systemic changes in higher education won't be found on the few dozen elite campuses but rather in the thousands of state universities and community colleges, many of them built in the last twenty years.

It is there that the world is changing. It is there that the walls of the ivory tower dissolve into the larger community, into the messy world of mass society. The future of higher education in this country lies not in Cambridge or Palo Alto, but at LA Pierce college in Canoga Park, at Long Island University, and in thousands of one- and two-story industrial concrete buildings where millions of immigrants, middle-aged women, and lower-middle-class students are trying to obtain the degree that they hope will give them that ineluctable edge in the thrivingly insecure economy of the United States today.[5]

In six years of graduate school at Harvard, I managed not to notice what was going on. Perhaps I was unusually myopic, but after conversations with hundreds of graduate students and professors, I think it is more accurate to say that I was raised in a myopic culture, the culture of elite, Ph.D. granting universities that manufacture the majority of today's professors and that enjoy the preponderance of media and popular attention.

In this elite culture, a graduate education in the humanities today differs remarkably little from that of twenty, thirty, or even fifty years ago. Graduate school is the womb of scholarship, where nascent academics are nurtured. Following a nineteenth-century German model, graduate schools stress scholarship. They are the first step a young scholar takes toward membership in an intellectual guild devoted to the preservation and production of knowledge.[6] Though other professional guilds have weakened, academic guilds are still strong. Each discipline, from history to physics, comparative literature to astronomy, has a professional organization that determines how work ought to be done, what ought to be rewarded, and which individuals ought to be tenured. The rules and requirements established by these guilds make it difficult, if not impossible, for academics to speak to audiences other than their professional peers. Historians and English professors use theories and field-specific jargon to answer arcane and often field-specific questions. Writing for the nonspecialist is not valued by the guild. Indeed, young academics who write about Abe Lincoln or affirmative action for a newspaper or magazine, let alone a book for a popular audience on these subjects, may even be penalized in the form of slow promotion or no promotion.

The result is a world of scholarship detached from the world that most of these scholars will actually inhabit. A ran-

dom few will land jobs in the Ivy League, but the vast majority will not. The former will glide into their professorial lives;
the latter will find themselves in very different surroundings,
employed as teachers of students coming from different
classes and having different agendas. There is a great divide
between Canoga Park and Cambridge, and it is one that few
graduate students and fewer professors know how to cross.

It is not that professors do not care, or that they are insen-
sitive to the needs of their students. Some are, certainly. But
far more are simply alienated, both from their students and
from the society in which they live, because of the increasing
professionalization of their academic training. This is particularly problematic in the humanities. Scientists and mathe-
maticians, classicists and economists, study subjects that
demand a level of expertise gained only after years of training. While there is a public need for some scientists to explain
science in terms that a nonscientist can understand, a wall
separates the language and concepts of science from those of
everyday life.

Yet, for subjects in the humanities like history, literature,
art, race, and gender, there is an ongoing public debate.
Questions that humanists pose have a public sphere. A
lawyer, for instance, is unlikely to go home and try to prove a
math theorem, whereas he might well pour himself a glass of
wine, take off his shoes, and read about Abraham Lincoln. A
doctor is unlikely to spend her lunch hour in the hospital
cafeteria reading Herodotus in the original Greek, but she
may well debate with other residents plans to cut affirmative
action.

The public sphere of the humanities is much wider and broader than the public sphere of science. Yet, academic humanists eschew the public sphere in favor of the academic. Rather than apply their knowledge to pressing political and social debates of the day, they attend to questions and issues that interest other academics. Some exceptional individuals bridge audiences, but the reward structure and socialization of graduate school and of the profession in general is such that crossing the divide remains the exception.

The culture of academia not only removes professors from the ebb and flow of the larger society that surrounds them; it also creates divisions between professors and their students. Take for example Kathi Kern, a young thirty-something woman who earned her Ph.D. in history from the University of Pennsylvania. In a job market where it is typical for more than 300 people to apply for one job, she was fortunate enough to be hired as an assistant professor at the University of Kentucky. The focus of her graduate study was women's history, and she spent years researching and writing a several-hundred-page dissertation on Elizabeth Cady Stanton and the Bible. At Kentucky, however, she was expected to teach the basic U.S. history survey, rather than courses on women in nineteenth-century America.

Her inclination at first was "to gender the survey." For every great man, she added and at times substituted a great woman. To the fiery William Lloyd Garrison, she juxtaposed the subject of her dissertation, Elizabeth Cady Stanton. In lieu of what she thought of as traditional white male history, she was going to expose her students to a panoply of women heroes. Instead of male Progressive reformers, she taught her students about Jane Addams. She was going to show them the central role of gender, with Ida Wells, Rosie the Riveter, and Lizzie Borden, and in the end, she hoped to provide her students with "an alternate narrative of the American past."

There was only one problem. Her students hated the course, and came close to hating her.

"When I taught my first course," she recalled, "the students walked out; they told me I wasn't teaching real American history; they gave me terrible student evaluations." They were hostile to the curriculum, and made their displeasure known in every way that they could.

To her credit, she realized that the fault lay with her. She learned from that first year that the values of graduate school clash with the values of most undergraduates. What makes perfect sense in a dissertation, in a graduate seminar, or at an academic conference may be incomprehensible to a college student.

Any profession, of course, has a level of knowledge that is simply nonsense to those outside the profession. Listen to doctors discussing a patient, engineers discussing a building, or telephone repairmen talking about cables. The same is true for academia. Phrases like "the social construction of gender" may be gibberish to most people on the street, but they are common jargon in the university.[7] Just as patients rightly protest when their doctor uses professional jargon to describe what's wrong, so too students object to language and frameworks that they don't understand. And just as many doctors only with great difficulty learn to communicate with their patients, so too do professors have difficulty communicating with their students.

But it goes beyond language. The students who walked out on Kathi Kern were not just objecting to language and concepts. They were objecting to a value system that they didn't share and to a professor whose disrespect for their values was evident. Professor Kern, educated in an elite school in the Northeast, intentionally devalued the traditional history that her Kentucky students had been taught in high school, because she believed that "the traditional narrative was problematic." That history may have been dominated by white men; it may even have mythologized the American past and glossed over oppression and conflict in U.S. history. But for her students, it also provided heroes, and stories that could inspire.

To her credit, Professor Kern learned that to teach students at a state school in Kentucky, she had to balance questions of gender and race with the traditional narratives of American history. "It was," she admitted, "quite an awakening."[8]

What was going on here? Why had Kathi Kern's advisers at the University of Pennsylvania led her to believe that the world outside of the Ivy League was waiting eagerly for this new message she had been empowered to deliver? Why had so many of her students rejected a "gendered" survey of the American past? Is this the way college education should play out, with teachers unsure of what they should be teaching and students defining by their reactions to what is offered them what it is they think they should be taught?

Was it always this way? To some degree. Professors have always pursued knowledge, and much of what is considered knowledge is arcane. Scholastic scholars of the Middle Ages tried to figure out how many angels could fit on the head of a pin, and the questions asked by professors today are often equally obscure. But until recently, the peculiarities of academic guilds mattered less to society at large. Ivy League professors engaged in complicated philosophical issues at the turn of the century catered to students who attended college less for the skills acquired in the classroom than for the social cache attached to the degree.

Today, however, professors are being asked to educate everyone, not just the elite. It is certainly true that the post-1960s professoriate tends not to share the traditional values of the economic and political elites; hence the accusation by conservative critics that the university has been taken over by "tenured radicals." However, the professoriate as a whole doesn't really embrace radicalism. Once again, the problem is the culture of academia. It is the academic culture of Kathi Kern's advisers at Penn that leads graduate students to delve into questions that do not pertain to the lives of most undergraduates or most Americans.

The story of Kathi Kern is but one example of the various contests that are occurring, contests that resemble a game of tug of war. Within the university itself, there is a tug of war to determine what should go on in the classroom. As millions of students from very different backgrounds meet in the university, they have begun to redefine the classroom. That is one reason for the proliferation of multicultural studies. Students demand to learn about themselves. When only young, affluent white men attended college, the white male curriculum went unchallenged. Now, every Latino, African American, Asian American, Irish American, woman, gay, and ad infinitum wants to learn about his or her roots. It is not always professors leading the way, as some conservative critics would have the public believe. Very often, it is reluctant administrators responding to student demands.

And a tug of war within academic guilds goes on among professors. That struggle is currently being won by those who support the model of the professor developed a century ago, refined in this century and then cemented by the system of tenure. Tenure is the ultimate guarantee not just of academic freedom, but of the independent power of the professoriate to set the terms of their own employment. In a time when public monies were more than adequate to meet the needs of higher education, the system of tenure worked. A young graduate student could be relatively sure that after several years of study at one of the handful of doctorate-granting universities a job as an assistant professor would be waiting. All that he had to do was follow the lead of an advisor and produce work that more or less conformed to the norms of the field.

Today, that system is in total disarray. Far more Ph.D. students are admitted and earn their degrees than the academic job market can possibly employ. Administrators at hundreds of schools create new graduate programs in the hopes of attracting more tuition money and enhancing the reputation of their schools knowing full well the slim prospects ahead for their graduates. And the hundreds of community colleges, underfunded by state legislatures, employ graduate students and Ph.D.'s at something that amounts to little more than starvation wages with no health benefits.

Tenure has so distorted the academic labor market that any benefits to free speech are more than outweighed by the distortions in the economy of higher education and the stultifying intellectual and professional orthodoxies that tenure promotes. This book suggests that tenure is not an absolute good, and in some situations, it does harm. Most professors believe that tenure is to be defended at all costs. Yet, in a world of more than 3,500 colleges, with millions of students and thousands of different needs, no one model of academic employment and no one definition of academic work would be suitable.

The problem is not tenure per se. It is the unthinking defense of tenure and the blind refusal to support alternate models and different structures. Academic guilds champion both intellectual orthodoxy and structural stasis, yet at hundreds of schools around the country, professors, administrators, and students are experimenting with new structures and changing definitions. The failure to embrace and even encourage these innovations is surely one of the great failings of academia today.

This book, then, offers both a road map to higher education today and some criticisms of the status quo. Some of the issues discussed in the pages that follow are unique to the humanities, but many are not, particularly questions of graduate education, tenure, and adjuncting. All of these issues are complicated. Many people both within and without the university have grappled with them, and the fact that questions such as tenure and the purpose of college remain unresolved is a testament to their complexity. Rather than presenting a detailed discussion of the pros and cons of any particular solution, this book suggests that positive changes will come only when professors, students, and the larger society abandon their search for one definition of higher education, one articulation of the humanities, and one ideal model of the scholar.

I have tried as much as possible to let the various participants in this tug of war describe their experiences in their own words. The struggles are waged by real people, with their own perspectives and their own voices, replete with ambiguity and complexity. I hope that this book, and the stories of professors and students grappling with these issues, will help clarify what college is for and what the various players think it is for. And I hope also that it will spur a complacent, troubled profession to apply its intellectual energies to these debates.

WHAT'S COLLEGE FOR?

1

THE
STUDENTS

So who are these students? Who are these undergraduates who jockey for control of the classroom?

The image of the college student in popular culture is still that of a white, athletic, young, and affluent person. That image is still largely accurate at Ivy League schools, at the most exclusive private colleges, and at places like Vanderbilt in Tennessee, Southern Methodist University in Dallas, the University of Chicago, or Stanford. But once you leave the manicured lawns of these hundred or so select institutions, that image breaks down. The students become older. They have jobs and kids. They are women, and immigrants, and minorities, and they are often paying their own way through college.

Students are not passive recipients of their education. More than ever, they shape what goes on in the classroom, what is taught, and how much they will spend on their schooling. In their efforts, individually and collectively, intentionally and inadvertently, to mold the classroom and the university to meet their needs, they often encounter professors who have rather different goals. Professors believe that a college diploma represents the culmination of an education. Students, however, increasingly see the diploma as a credential that will lead to a better job. In an ideal world, education and credentializing would be compatible, but in the world of higher education today, they are often at odds.

In a country with thousands of schools spread across thousands of miles, no student is typical. Outside of the elite schools, student attitudes are so diverse as to defy most generalizations. To begin with, schools in different parts of the country reflect their region. Much as people in Mississippi approach life somewhat differently from people in Manhattan, state schools have agendas that mirror the local populace. A state school in Minnesota is likely to have courses on Scandinavian literature, and Swedish language courses might draw a healthy enrollment, whereas in Texas, the Mexican American War and the Alamo attract interest. These state schools, whether they are four-year universities or two-year community colleges, account for more than three-quarters of all enrollments, and they draw students primarily from their surrounding areas. A large majority of students at UT-Austin are from Texas; most students at Berkeley are from California; and the University of Minnesota is composed mostly of Minnesotans.

That in turn leads to variations in student life. Consider the following episode: On October 14, 1996, an odd event took place at Texas A&M University, in College Station. This event attracted little attention. In fact, it hardly even rated a story in *The Battalion*, the student campus newspaper. Each day, the paper runs a column called "Debriefing," which consists of half a dozen short paragraphs reporting miscellaneous happenings. On October 24, the third paragraph told of this event the week before.

Surgery Result of Possible KA Hazing

A member of the Kappa Alpha Order had a testicle surgically removed as a result of a possible hazing incident on Oct. 14.

The University Police Department referred the case to the Brazos County Sheriff's Department.

Officials say the case is currently under investigation by the Department of Student Affairs.[1]

It is hard to imagine a missing testicle receiving so little attention in the Northeast, or in the West. It is also hard to imagine the aforementioned orb occasioning no more than a perfunctory mention at a small college. Were such an episode to occur at Williams College, in rural Massachusetts, or at Macalester, in St. Paul, it would no doubt be emblazoned across the student newspaper in bold type, and it might even make the local evening news. In fact, in the fall of 1997, a student at the Massachusetts Institute of Technology, in Cambridge, went to a frat party, drank until he passed out, went into a coma, and died. The story appeared on the front page of not just *The Boston Globe* but the nationally circulated *New York Times* as well.[2]

In College Station, however, a missing testicle was buried on the second page of the campus newspaper, after stories on the

Internet, a student program to clean church parking lots, Halloween plans, and a student winning $50,000 in a national cooking contest sponsored by *Good Housekeeping* magazine.

These episodes demonstrate that the social mores of students and their schools are as diverse as they are in the population as a whole. But while diversity characterizes student life, what goes on in the classroom is less dependent on the region. Specific course offerings may differ, but the teaching goals are remarkably uniform. A history course in one part of the country is very much like a history course in another. This national culture of classroom education has evolved over decades, and one reason for the continuity is that professors are drawn from a wider geographic net than the community of students. They are also drawn from a small intellectual community. A professor of English in Texas almost certainly has had the same training as a professor of English in Maryland, and they are likely to teach the texts in roughly similar fashion.

Beyond the professors, however, the type of school matters greatly. Teaching Mark Twain may be similar at two elite schools in different parts of the country, but not at a major university and a community college in the same city, because the students at the elite schools are better prepared, more accustomed to the workload, and tend to have more time to devote to their studies than students at second-tier state schools and community colleges. They have more time because they are more affluent and as a result are not under the same pressures to hold down a job while getting their degree. Kathi Kern's initial problems at the University of Kentucky point to the cultural fault line between elite schools and the rest of American higher education.

At the elite schools, undergraduates approach their studies with a sense of entitlement. Of the hundreds of students I taught at Harvard and Dartmouth, I'm relatively sure that it never occurred to a single one of them not to go to college. Whether they are the product of prep schools or of public high schools, all were high achievers who were told by parents, teachers, college guidance counselors, or their friends that college lay on the other side of their high school diploma. For these select thousands, college is simply the next in a series of stages leading to membership in productive society. For many, undergraduate years are themselves preparatory to some form of graduate school, whether in law, business, medicine, or academia. For these students, college is just what one does, as automatic as sex, marriage, child rearing, and buying a home.

For millions of others, however, college is a choice. It is not a natural choice, not a choice parents made or friends are making, not a choice available in their country of origin, and it is not a choice without sacrifice—of time, of pride, and most of all, of money, which means that many of these students are working, some at full-time jobs. They take evening classes, one or two at a time, in order to earn their bachelor's degrees in five or six years. They juggle family, job, and school. They have mortgages to pay, and they have decided to spend some of their money to acquire skills, job skills.

For these students, college is a commodity. Elite students essentially view their experience as an entitlement. Not so for the millions of others at community colleges and state schools. In the 1990s alone, the average debt burden for a college student grew from $8,200 to $18,800. Given that these students, once they graduate, tend to earn between $20,000 and $30,000 a year, those debts are heavy, and some schools have begun efforts to limit borrowing by students. In addition to loans, three-quarters of all students work part-time during the school year, and more than 15 percent work full-time.[3] For their money, for their investment, for the hours they work in order to pay for their classes, these students expect to be taught something they don't already know. They expect to learn. And at the end, they expect to get a better job, more pay, and a better life.

Job concerns occupy all college students, from the most elite to those at the most down-at-the-heels community college. In contrast to students of the 1960s, who, when surveyed about their goals, routinely answered that they wanted to make the world a better place, today's students are far more likely to say that their goal is jobs, jobs, jobs. In a recent survey, 75 percent of college students said that being well off was their primary goal, as opposed to 40 percent who hoped to use their college years to develop a meaningful philosophy of life. A college degree has always been perceived as a ticket to a better life, but never before has it been so perceived as a ticket to a better career.[4] Recently, lawmakers in Kentucky, Virginia, and West Virginia have talked of redesigning public universities in their states in order to prepare their students to enter the work force. "If we don't focus on getting people the skills they need to get a job, then we have missed the point," said former West Virginia governor Gasper Caperton.[5]

The driving pressure to obtain a degree is reflected in every bookstore and every newsstand. Each fall, *Time, U.S. News & World Report, Newsweek,* the *New York Times,* and countless other newspapers and magazines run special editions or include supplements about how to get in. The ultrahip *Rolling Stone* now comes out with its annual college issue; the 1997 version exposed questionable curricula at journalism schools, offered a profile of an innovative business professor, and slammed the ranking system of *U.S. News & World Report.*[6] In light of the increased concern about cost, *Boston Magazine* reported on which colleges provide the most bang for the buck and which are "rip-offs."[7] It may be only a matter of time before *Consumer Reports* comes out with a survey of best and worst values. And if the magazines aren't enough, there's shelf after shelf of how-to books at every Borders and Barnes & Noble. Simon & Schuster publishes more than a dozen *Newsweek* and Stanley Kaplan guides; *Barron's* prints its report on every college in the United States; and there are also guides to graduate school.

For most students, getting into the local state university or community college is not the issue. Rather, it is staying in, and paying up. The majority of colleges in the United States admit well over half of their applicants, and in most states, the public university system is designed to accommodate any citizen of the state who wishes to attend college. The reality for most students is less romantic than popular images suggest. Regina Lark, for instance, worked full-time as an administrative assistant at CalState Northridge while getting her B.A. Or take Jennifer at Ohio State: "As an undergraduate, I worked between thirty-five and forty-five hours a week at a grocery store. I did not do this to pay for a sports car; I did this to pay for school and a place to live." Or Lise at a community college in New York, who is a full-time student and a full-time instructional aide in the public school system. Or Carrie, a student at the University of Albany, who cannot help but reflect on the economic strain: "College tuitions are on the rise nationally; thus each year what a student spends in school is greatly increasing their debt. You cannot receive financial aid if you are attending part-time. But you can't even get an entry-level job doing anything interesting without a bachelor's degree. So where are we working? Well, erotic dancing, bartending, and waiting tables. I'd rather not spend fifteen years of my life like this waiting to get the first degree of many; I can spend the next ten years paying off the debt."

Then there's the course work. Out of the four courses and two hundred students in Carrie's classes, only sixteen have the luxury of simply being students. If you take four courses a term as a full-time student, it takes at least thirty hours a week, with class time, reading, test preparation, assignments. Add that to a thirty- to forty-hour work week. Said Carrie grimly, "Someone I know joked about letting sleep be the thing that goes. Well, basically it is. At a cost to the professor of a lively, awake, functioning student. How are we to remember what we've read, or stay awake through a three-hour course?"[8]

It's true that today's students are not the first to work their way through college. The Ivies of yesteryear always had a two-class system of those paying their way and those on insufficient scholarships who had to work for room and board.

You can still find lawyers who put themselves through law school at night.

But while the dilemma of balancing work and school isn't new, the financial burden of college today makes the process far more daunting. At the elite schools, it would be nearly impossible for a student to earn enough to underwrite four years of classes. At $30,000 a year in tuition plus room and board, the cost of elite schools surpasses the annual income of most Americans.[9]

The average cost for tuition and fees at a four-year college in 1996 was nearly $13,000 at private schools and over $3,000 at public universities. At the better state schools, in-state tuition, housing, and fees top $10,000—certainly more manageable but still costly. And at community colleges and extension classes at public and private universities, the cost of a course ranges from as little as $400 to over $2,000.[10]

If you have a fairly typical income of $25,000, spending even $1,600 to $1,800 a year on classes and books is a considerable expenditure. That gets even more considerable if there are kids to feed, health insurance to pay for, and a mortgage. More often than not, students pay in excess of $1,800 a year, and the only way they can afford the cost is to take out loans. The current trend to make some or all of federally guaranteed student loans tax deductible tends to gloss over the question of school indebtedness altogether.[11]

The financial burden is considerable, and it is one that an ever increasing number of students confront. With heavy debts and part-time jobs that occupy a significant portion of the week, student life rarely resembles our images of college as a special four years removed from the pressures of the adult world. But more than that, these economic realities create a new set of priorities, ones that at best coexist uneasily with traditional higher education.

At school after school, commodification trumps education. While enrollments in business and communications courses expand, the humanities suffer, because few people see any link between the humanities and the skills necessary for success in the modern economy. Leaving college with heavy debts, students feel constrained in their choice of careers. "People feel that classes in the humanities are useless because they do not directly apply to a job in such fields as medicine, science, etc., that make money," sighed Elizabeth, an undergraduate at UC-Santa Barbara. "I know that I will not make a lot of money teaching high-school history, but I will love my job. I will have a sense of purpose. I will know that by teaching children about our country and the world that I will be helping create a generation of good citizens." With ten, twenty, thirty thousand dollars of debt, careers in business become essential, while careers as teachers, social workers, or others in the nonprofit sector become less viable even though they remain important to society.

In addition to creating a potential dearth of young people who plan to pursue socially imperative but less remunerative careers, the current economics of higher education leads undergraduates and their parents to approach college as consumers and not simply as students.[12] This can have a positive effect. Students who are paying their own way tend not to take their education for granted. But the downside is more troubling. Students who take the stance of consumers have an expectation that they are buying a product, namely, a college degree. If a hundred credits are required for that degree, and each credit costs $100, then a college degree costs $10,000. In order to obtain that degree, they have to receive a passing grade, and often a C or above, in their courses.

The result is predictable. When students do not receive the grade they need to pass, they often hold the professor and then the administration responsible. Students have been known to march into a dean's office and demand that a particular teacher be fired for giving grades that are "too low." They have been known to give teachers poor evaluations for "assigning too much reading." They have refused to do work beyond that which they feel they ought to do. And all because of the presumption that in return for their money, they ought to receive the degree.

In many places, students are trying to redefine their own workload. A professor at the University of Utah tells a story of students complaining to an associate dean after they were asked to take essay exams instead of multiple choice. Students at Grambling State University in Louisiana and at the University of Northern Arizona have sued their schools in court for failing to provide a quality education. One student called his school "a diploma mill" and derided the poor teaching skills of the faculty.[13] One teacher observed of the students at her school that "there is considerable polarization in our classes between those students who are here for an education and those who are here for a degree." At conferences, professors often tell stories of students who not only refuse to learn certain facts of history or to read novels assigned in class but who aggressively defend their unwillingness to absorb these things on the grounds that they know their career paths and hence they know what knowledge they do and do not need.

Add to this mix the economic burden most campuses operate under. While Ivy League schools have the luxury of admitting one in ten of their applicants, most colleges must scramble for enrollment. The need for student tuition dollars gives students an added advantage in their struggles with teachers. Deans will be less likely to support faculty when there is a glut of qualified teachers and a dearth of qualified students. The distorted supply and demand of the academic job market has a number of negative consequences, which we will examine more in subsequent chapters. But faced with the prospects of students withdrawing, or with student protests against teachers creating bad PR for a school, deans appear increasingly willing to censure faculty and concede to student demands, however unreasonable.[14]

Although there are no reliable studies on the reading workload of students, anecdotal evidence suggests that students are doing less reading than ever before. Students will no longer read what they used to. Comparing syllabi from thirty years ago with those of today, it's clear that reading assignments are much lighter than they once were. Too much can be made of this. After all, students have been using Cliffs Notes and other "condensed" sources, including *Reader's Digest* books, for quite some time.[15] But students are now more vocal in their refusal to read beyond a very limited number of pages, as little as thirty to forty pages a week in some courses. Students offer a variety of excuses, but the most difficult one to counter is the claim that they simply don't have the time. If they are working a full-time job and caring for a family, then several hundred pages a week in each of three or four courses can become untenable.

At the same time, students, like most human beings, don't necessarily like to work. Fear of failure may not be the best motivator, but it is often an effective one. Knowing that you will be evaluated negatively if you do not do the required work is a spur to doing it. If, however, students use both appeals to administrators and harsh teacher evaluations, and if the nature of academic employment now means that these are effective tools to put pressure on professors, then the ability of a professor to get students to do the work is hampered.

Some professors resort to the most juvenile, hand-holding techniques to get their students to read. Some go as far as reading out loud to their students on the theory that otherwise they'll never do the assignment. Others trim more and more pages off their syllabi each year. The result is that in many places education is, in effect, "dumbed down."

This "dumbing down" is particularly prevalent in the humanities, where the courses are harder to justify to students and parents, both of whom view college almost entirely in job-oriented terms. One business major at Southern Methodist University told me that she took an occasional English course in order to give herself a break from numbers. Most of her friends, however, couldn't understand why she bothered. At SMU, the business school is awash in money, and the connections between it and the Dallas business community are well established. Many students go to SMU to major in business, join a fraternity or sorority, and then find a good entry-level position through the contacts they've made in their four years. Humanities courses are seen as a luxury at best, and for many they're simply a waste of time.

Many schools still have a humanities requirement, whether it is the American Cultures curriculum at UC-Berkeley or the state-mandated U.S. history survey at all public colleges in Texas, and the students I talked to by and large support the notion that some exposure to history and literature is an essential part of their education. For Vina Ha, an undergraduate at Berkeley majoring in Asian American studies and sociology, the humanities matter a great deal, but his parents disagree. "My parents were Vietnamese immigrants in 1975, having fled from the south. I think that there's a distinct cultural difference between me as second-generation Vietnamese American. There is a cultural rift between me and my parents. Their goal for me is to work as hard as possible. They want me to be in the money field. My brother's a lawyer, but they see the degree as a means of economic advancement. Money is the only thing they see in the United States that's of value."

Vina said that he plans to go to graduate school and get a Ph.D. I asked how his parents felt about his choice of major. "If I told my parents that I was going to major in film, or not go after a postgraduate degree and just stay in humanities as an undergrad, they might have a hard time with that because it might hinder my chances of becoming successful money-

wise. But I'm doing ethnic studies because of the obvious social and economic inequality that I've seen in society."

Vina sounded like an idealistic student of the 1960s. He
talked about wanting to help society rather than making
money, but he was uncomfortable with the tendency of his
professors to overtheorize about important social issues. "If I
immerse myself in the theories too much," he said, "I remove
myself from the people I'm trying to help. I'm interested in
public policy, but going into academia would probably remove me from the masses. I'm interested in helping the
masses and speaking to them. If I go into academia and write
highly academic books, then I remove myself from the very
people I care most about."

Still, something about academia attracted Vina. "If I go
into academia, I'm arming myself with information, bettering
myself, but hopefully I'll stick with my goal. The point of humanities courses is to broaden people's awareness of other
cultures, of American history."

Vina pauses for a moment. He's an undergraduate teaching
assistant in one of the American Cultures courses. All Berkeley
undergraduates are required to take one of the courses, regardless of their major. "If you have a a guy majoring in science," Vina continued, "he's going to flake off on the reading,
and just try to pass. So he's going to come away with less than
others. He'll be able to describe things, but not analyze them.
Still, a little taste of the humanities is better than nothing."

Two students at UT-Austin told me that they thought their
course comparing U.S. slavery with Russian serfdom was the
best thing they were taking, and both of them were freshmen

who didn't plan to major in the humanities. One student gushed that she talked to her father about the course constantly and that she was surprised at how much the course made her think about not just the past but also the world around her. Other students emphasized that history courses got them to think about contemporary politics and social controversies. A student in an ethnic studies course at Berkeley wrote in an evaluation, "Knowing the history of this country, in terms of governmental policy towards minority groups, is very valuable. This class made me aware and provided me with a strong foundation on which to base my opinions and actions for the future." Another wrote, "To understand the actions of other states internationally, we must comprehend ourselves, know our history as well as theirs, and we need to learn from the past accomplishments and failures of this nation."[16]

Much of the public discussion over the humanities has focused on the content of these courses. The multicultural slant of Berkeley's core and similar programs at places like SUNY-Binghamton[17] have been the target of conservative assaults on the forces of relativism and political correctness. That in turn has led to a series of rebuttals by those defending multiculturalism as a simple reflection of racial and ethnic realities in America today. These arguments are couched in almost apocalyptic terms, as if American civilization will rise and fall depending on whether students learn multicultural, minority history rather than traditional "great men" history.[18]

What the debate misses is not only that it is rarely a case of learning multicultural history *instead of* traditional history, but that the greater danger is that students will learn no history and literature at all. Berkeley students, for all the supposed radicalism of the curriculum, enter traditional professions once they graduate and become active and successful members of society. The same is true for students at Austin, or at Texas A&M, where the curriculum more closely resembles what it used to be.

Humanities at best teach students how to think critically. They do not teach students what to think, and few professors are ideological enough to try to force students to adopt a party line one way or another. When students feel that they are being pressured, as in the case of Kathi Kern's first class at Kentucky, they let the teacher know, and they usually succeed in deterring professors from embarking on an ideological crusade.

The capacity to read analytically and the ability to write clearly are two of the most valuable skills any would-be job seeker can have. More than courses on accounting or communications, humanities courses can teach these skills. In addition, they do offer students a grounding in their culture and in their past that enables them to relate to and make sense of the world around them—that allows them to evaluate political candidates, to read or listen to the news without blindly accepting what they are told, to make the case for a particular social issue that they hold dear, and to engage in debate with others who do not share their views.[19]

While content does matter, it doesn't matter as much as cultural ideologues of the right or the left suggest. In that respect, it is truly better, as Vina Ha said, to have some exposure to history and culture than none at all. Which is not to suggest that content is meaningless. As I went from class to class in college after college, I began to notice that the pendulum has swung too far. Process has trumped content in the humanities, and if that continues, then there will be no critical thinking.

In education schools throughout the country, the process-content debate rages. Some educators insist that education consists of content and that selecting content is the most consequential decision that a professor can make. Other demur and argue that in a diverse society the most appropriate goal revolves around process. To some extent, those who stress content are allied with those who defend the traditional college curriculum. Yet the process-content issue also has an inside baseball dimension, one which animates education professionals yet is opaque if you're not one of them.

Outside of professional educators, the consensus appears to be that a certain minimum level of content is necessary if process is to have any rigor. Students, however, are far more comfortable with process. It's easier to discuss your opinions, to engage in arguments over pressing issues of affirmative action or crime, than it is to master a text or remember what happened when. As the power balance shifts away from professors and toward students, the emphasis on process is becoming more pronounced.

The process-content debate occurs at every level from kindergarten through graduate school, but in college itself, a particular dynamic seems at work. Professors, some of whom gave little or no thought to teaching while they were earning their doctoral degrees, find themselves plopped in front of a class and told to teach. When they start lecturing in sonorous tones about arcane theories of literature or obscure historiographical controversies, they notice that their students' eyes glaze over. But when they read a passage out loud and ask their students what they think, or when they spark debate about slavery in the nineteenth century by asking the students about race relations at the end of the twentieth, their students become more animated.

Some of those techniques are useful, but only as an entry point to a more substantive discussion about the text or subject of the course. Often, however, they become a substitute for serious consideration of difficult issues. As students resist the impetus to work harder, and as professors find themselves at an increasing disadvantage in this tug-of-war with their charges, classes often stop at the starting point. That has given rise to charges that the classroom now resembles a confessional: Personal experience dominates the discussions.[20]

Still, some of the changes brought on by student demands are positive. A curriculum that includes issues of race and gender provides a deeper and more complete understanding of our society, which is indeed filled with nonwhites and women. An attempt by professors to engage students actively is an improvement over the rote learning of days past and over the passive student dutifully taking notes and then promptly forgetting everything once the course is over. But the pressure that students exercise to reduce workloads and to steer away from content is not healthy. Courses only succeed in inculcating critical thought if they are rigorous. Each statement has to be assessed, tested, and often challenged. Being rewarded simply for voicing an opinion is not a recipe for critical thought.

As a group, professors seem at sea in the face of this challenge. Students do not act as a unified whole. Economic pressures and very human inclinations to do less rather than more work go a long way toward explaining why they demand what they do. An expectation to learn about themselves in language that makes sense to them leads students to reject both rigid ideology and brittle academic theory. While politicians, parents, and pundits can exhort students to behave differently, it's unlikely that any cohesive shift will occur in a student population nearing 16 million.

The professoriate, however, is defined. Professors exist in a finite professional community, and they devote considerable attention to figuring out what they should be doing. They have written and unwritten rules of conduct and a hierarchy of promotion and rewards. Professional organizations exist to bring practitioners together and to establish the guidelines for admittance and success. In short, professors constitute a guild. As such, they have a corporate identity. Students cannot be expected to deliberate goals and issues and en masse alter their behavior. Only professors can.

But before discussing how these professors came to be who they are and what motivates them and animates them, we should pause for a moment. Generalizations have their place, but only if we understand what we are generalizing about. Students, professors, and the classroom share an intimate experience. On average, a student taking a class listens and speaks with the professor for at least thirty hours in a semester. That thirty hours of focused time is more contact than many of us have with close friends during the same twelve-week period. Each class has its own particular rhythm, and out of hundreds of thousands of classes, some generalizations do emerge.

The debates over higher education tend to be waged in the calm and clarity of the abstract. In World War I, French and British generals sat in their châteaux and moved armies on clean maps while the soldiers confronted the confusing challenges of the front. The terrain mapped out by many of the culture-war literati is difficult to find in the real classrooms of America.

Before going any further, therefore, let's take a moment to peek behind the classroom door.

2

THE CLASSROOM

The sun streams through the window, cascading off of the dark mahogany chairs. The professor speaks, asks a question, the students nod thoughtfully, and a few tentatively raise their hands to speak. Later, with knapsacks dangling from one shoulder, the students swirl out the main door of the building, brimming with enthusiasm.

It's a generic scene, endlessly repeated on television and in the movies. It is almost stock footage, so familiar is it. At times, it even resembles reality, but there's more texture, more complexity, and more variety than popular images suggest. What follows is a series of sketches, each in its way representative of different classroom dynamics: a U.S. history course at a community college outside of Los Angeles, another at a land-grant university in Texas, and a large lecture on American education at the University of California. The three professors represent a cross section as well: one a "nontraditional" graduate student, one an established scholar, and another a professor-cum-activist. These three episodes expose separate facets of higher education, alternate approaches to history and culture, and distinct philosophies of teaching. Yet, there are similarities as well, parallel difficulties, and some troubling trends.

Twilight in Canoga Park. Just north of Los Angeles over the Santa Monica Mountains, the valley sprawls with seemingly endless one-story houses. In one of these, Regina Lark lives with her husband and her dogs.

Regina is an adjunct professor at the local community college. She has closely cropped dark hair. She smokes. Her face is careworn, but her eyes are lively. She doesn't look like a professor, but then Los Angeles Pierce Community College looks nothing like the campuses most of us picture in our minds. In fact, it looks like an industrial park, and not a particularly impressive one: low shanties, in rows, and a sprawling parking lot for the cars of the commuter students and their commuter teachers.

Regina is also a graduate student. She is deep in the throes of her dissertation on Japanese war brides, which she is writing under the joint auspices of the history department and the women's studies program at the University of Southern California, one of the more affluent campuses in the Los Angeles area. Regina typifies a whole generation of graduate students and community college teachers. Her path to USC was not traditional. The first in her family to go to college, let alone get a graduate degree, she worked while taking a class or two per term for twelve years at Los Angeles Pierce College. Twelve years of night classes and day jobs. Then she moved up a notch in the California state system, to CalState-Northridge, where she worked forty hours a week as a clerical assistant in the history department while finishing her B.A. She wanted to be a high school teacher, but while working in the department, she realized that she could go further in her education. She enrolled in the master's program at Northridge, and then was admitted to the Ph.D. program at USC.

"I come from no educational background," she told me. "Nobody in my family has ever pursued this at all. So I didn't know what was what. I said, huh, the professors are working a couple of days a week and they're earning pretty decent salaries."

It wasn't easy for Regina. At each stage, she felt woefully unprepared. After attending an average, mediocre high school, community college was a challenge. But after she got the hang of it, it wasn't hard. The demands were minimal, and most of the tests were multiple choice. There was one downside. One of her English teachers just wanted to date her. "I was poor," she said, "so I let him take me out to dinner every Wednesday before class. I got straight As and never learned to write an essay."

Her first semester at Northridge, she got Cs. It devastated her, and she dropped out until she could learn to write. She did and then finished the degree. The University of Southern California offered an entirely new set of hurdles.

"It was a culture shock. I thought, 'I'm at the big kids' school now.' I was in a seminar with students who just seemed so much brighter than me, and they had had so many more educational opportunities than me. They had come from Ivy League schools, and they were ten years younger than me. They had parents who had degrees or were professionals, who had instilled this thirst for education. I felt totally out of my league. I soon found out that everyone was in the same position I was. Everybody was scared. Everybody thought everyone else was smarter."

No longer intimidated, she began the long and often arduous process of getting her Ph.D. She floated from advisor to advisor and finally found a woman who supported her plan to interview surviving Japanese war brides about their experiences. She had expected to be taught the crafts of research and teaching. She found, however, that there was much less of the latter than of the former.

"There's so much hype around this publish-or-perish scenario. What are schools here for except to teach others? I think that that gets lost in graduate school. I try to get advice from advisors, yet everybody's working on their big projects. I don't begrudge that, but they shouldn't take on graduate students. I don't want to be in the big schools and produce big work, but instead I want to be a teacher. I'm unusual among my peers in that I've been teaching my own courses. A lot of grad students haven't seen the greatness of being in a classroom, and when they do, some of them will change their attitudes. But I know that a lot of them want to go on to the big things, and there's not enough room up there in the Ivies for everybody. I think that discourages people, because that is held up as the goal. So we lose sight of what goes on in the classroom."

Few of her professors talked about teaching, and she was surprised at how intensely they focused on research and how little they attended to their graduate students, let alone the undergraduates. She had seen some of the same problems at Northridge, a middle-tier school that by legislative mandate emphasizes teaching. In Regina's words, "A place like Northridge is betwixt and between." Promotion depends in part on good teaching, but the professors are most passionate about their research. Much of the faculty were new Ph.D.'s in the 1960s, and when they were hired, they saw Northridge as a step toward a career at a prestigious research university.

Little did they know that the 1970s were the beginning of a decades-long job squeeze in higher education, which has only worsened in the 1990s. In the seventies, grim stories were told of cabbies in New York City with Ph.D.'s from Harvard. People hoped these stories were apocryphal; they weren't.

"So they got stuck there at Northridge," Regina observed, "and many of them see themselves as having been stuck. There are a handful of scholars there who continue to produce work, and there are those who haven't done original research and haven't stayed current in their field. They're teaching the same old tired courses. There's a lot of resentment. One woman I know hates the fact that she's there and not at some Ivy League institution."

Regina herself doesn't feel at ease researching and writing. She often has difficulty understanding articles she reads in academic journals and blames herself for lacking the skill to interpret academic rhetoric and jargon. She isn't comfortable with academic terms or academic analysis. She calls herself "plainspoken." If she weren't so determined to finish things she starts, she'd give up on her dissertation to focus on community college teaching full-time.

Regina makes no bones about bringing her views into the classroom. "I'm a die-hard radical feminist, and as much as I keep myself reeled in in the classroom, I can't help but allow my cynicism towards certain aspects of society enter into the dialogue. I just try to make it clear over and over again that though I feel very strongly about some things, those are just my opinions. I just did midterm evaluations, and one student said that issues of sex shouldn't be brought into the classroom. But I think these issues are part of our history. Somebody said I shouldn't cuss, but I wasn't even aware I did that."

What are we to make of someone like Regina? At once opinionated and unsure, radical but respectful of academic authority, a women's studies graduate student who teaches a traditional U.S. history survey, a married women in her late thirties doing what no one in her family has ever done, a graduate student at a good school who rejects the model of the researcher-professor and elects to teach instead?

There are thousands of Reginas across the country, though you wouldn't know it from most accounts of higher education. It's impossible to draw simple conclusions from her account. Does she represent the failure of her advisors to inculcate the proper values? Or is her quiet rejection of those values a testament to her? Is her self-proclaimed radicalism proof that academia is a den of liberalism? And does she successfully walk that fine line between advocating her political views in class and teaching her students the facts of the past?

Her class on modern American history at LA Pierce College straggles in at 7:00 in the evening. Many arrive late, especially since the buses are erratic. These are people who live in Los Angeles and use public transportation. They range in age from sixteen to over seventy. Married and divorced. Several are immigrants preparing for their citizenship exam; others are trying to earn their associate's degree in order to be eligible for a four-year B.A. at one of the CalState schools. A few others are there on a whim, just to learn a bit about American history.

Bob, in his seventies, with slightly stained pants and eczema, is going back to school in his retirement. He complains to me about his grandson and his children, who are clearly in the midst of family problems. The discussion is about Vietnam, and Bob preempts Regina a number of times with his personal memories. His comments are astute, and his recollection of events surprisingly accurate. He reflects on how much we have declined as a society, and that inadvertently sets off a debate on how much and how far.

After barely ten minutes specifically focusing on the Vietnam War, the discussion veers off to the more immediate concerns of the students and their lives. Regina encourages them to speak about their own experiences. The students are uniformly negative about society today. A striking high school student with precariously high-heeled clogs and kohl-dark eyebrows says evenly that drugs are ruining the schools, that kids don't respect authority, and that the death penalty is necessary to restore some sort of order.

As Vietnam recedes into the distance, Regina asks the rest of the class what they think about the death penalty. A dark-

haired, heavyset middle-aged woman talks of her Italian family and its strong values and then comments on how rare that
seems today. She seconds the notion that drugs are killing
kids and destroying families and talks of her worries about
her own children. She too thinks harsher punishments are
necessary, especially the death penalty. Soon there is a chorus of voices supporting longer jail terms, no parole, and
death for heinous criminals. For these students, across the
generations, Vietnam laid the seeds of moral decay, and only
law and family can save America.

An African immigrant in the class objects. In his country,
he says, there is only the law of a dictator, and death is frequently the punishment. In halting English, he chides his
classmates for not understanding that what makes America
different is freedom, the right to say and do what he feels like
saying and doing, without fear of death and imprisonment.

If Regina had any aspirations of converting her students to
her liberalism, she wasn't succeeding. Her students had their
own views, many of which were sharply at odds with hers. She
was their teacher, of American history, not of political or social
philosophy. They weren't there to listen to sermons or to the
proselytizing of a professor. To her credit, Regina expressed
her views and gave her students ample room to express theirs.

Yet the students were less interested in talking about history than about their lives and their opinions. So why were
they there, I wondered? Why American history? Most students go to community college for economic reasons: to enhance their earning potential, to get a better job, or to get to
a better college so that they can get a better job. Almost all of

Regina's students told me that a good job is their primary reason for going to college. They have been told by employers and parents that they need skills that only college can provide them—business skills and computer skills. So why were these very practical students taking a U.S. survey course on a weekday evening in Canoga Park?

For Bob and another student in his forties, it was a chance to reflect on some of what they had lived through. The course was like a reminder, a not always pleasant trip down memory lane. For the younger students, Vietnam is ancient history. One twenty-something said that taking the course helped him understand the present. Others nodded. "I think we need to know from where we came," one women said. "I think if you learn from mistakes in the past, it helps create a more disciplined society," added the high school student who had mounted a vigorous defense of the death penalty.

I pushed them further. What about job skills? How does knowing about the Tet offensive help someone get a job? Every one of them vigorously defended the utility of history. Some felt that unless they knew what had happened, they would never be able to form opinions about the world around them. Others thought that history helped them empathize with the experience of different groups. One Italian American woman said that though she had always understood what it meant to be Italian American, as a result of the class she "started to look at people in a different light. I start to see more about others."

Her mention of other cultures sparked discussion of common ground and shared history. Like so many history classes in college today, this one nurtured multiple perspectives rather than one grand synthetic narrative. The same students who moments before had bemoaned the loss of authority and the breakdown of society staunchly rejected the notion that "we" have a shared past.

"People say that Columbus discovered America," the high school student said. "But if people of other races or countries have learned it differently, then they're going to say no, he didn't. So history teaches you to appreciate different perspectives."

"Who would dictate what that one narrative or that one story would be?" asked a young man in the back. "Who would say what that one common interpretation should be? You need to learn to use your mind and make your own interpretation."

Regina agreed. "I think common background is a matter of interpretation. I teach a different commonality than many traditional teachers. What about the commonality that we're all a nation of immigrants? Someone else might say that our common background is that we all live under one Constitution. It's really subjective to whomever is putting the dialogue across. There's no consensus that Columbus discovered America anymore."

It was past 8:30, and the class ended. Cookies, chips, and soda made a rapid appearance, followed by a rapid disappearance. Same time next week, and then Watergate.

The discussion was disorganized, and the students clearly substituted opinions for hard thinking. Most of them probably had not done the assigned reading, and in the face of their resistance to detailed examination of what happened in

Vietnam, Regina engaged their passions. That made for a vibrant discussion, and the students clearly felt that they were learning something about each other and about life. Far from imposing her views, Regina acted as a facilitator for a wide-ranging debate about culture and its discontents.

The tension between often dry substance and the rough-and-tumble of opinions manifests itself constantly in classrooms throughout the country. So does the peculiar dynamic of liberal teacher and more conservative students. Halfway across the country from Canoga Park, Texas A&M University occupies an alternate universe. One of the grandest of the land-grant universities, Texas A&M is vast. Nearly fifty thousand students live in College Station, a hundred miles outside of Austin. The Aggies of A&M are very white and very traditional. They define themselves as everything the liberal book snobs at the University of Texas at Austin ain't. The Aggies are fiercely loyal to their sports teams, fiercely devoted to fraternities, and thoroughly focused on their future jobs in the grand ole state of Texas.

H. W. Brands teaches an honors U.S. history survey to about twenty-five of A&M's finest. The history department is in the Agriculture Building, a good indication of how prominent the humanities are in the Aggie universe. But the Texas state legislature requires all Texas college students to take two terms of U.S. history. During the cold war, it was thought that American students needed to know the glories of the American past to inoculate them against any communist propaganda. If you don't want to take two terms of U.S. history, you can't graduate college. There is one exception: Instead of the American survey, you can take Texas history for three terms.

Bill Brands is a tall, lean graduate of the University of Texas at Austin, with a trim mustache and goatee. Unlike Regina Lark, Brands is a full professor and the author of numerous books, mostly on U.S. foreign policy. Though he has tenure at Texas A&M, he lives in Austin and makes the hundred-mile commute each way twice a week. His honors class on this particular day is discussing the Constitution, and, this being Texas, it isn't long before the conversation turns to the Second Amendment and the right to bear arms.

The sentiment of the class is strongly in favor of the right of U.S. citizens to own however many guns they choose. Opinion is divided over whether the type of arms can be regulated, and most students agree that there should be a waiting period such as the one mandated by the Brady bill.

Brands leans back in his chair and probes the limits of this right. Though he is to the political left of his students on this issue, he encourages them to speak, whatever their views. With a mischievous gleam in his eye, he asks them about guns on campus. He wants to see how far their gun libertarianism goes.

The students think for a moment, and several chime in that it's certainly within the purview of campus officials to limit guns in class or at sporting events. "After all," one student says seriously, "you couldn't even carry guns into saloons in the Old West."

I had arranged with Brands to take some of the class time to talk with the students alone. I ask them if it is a waste of their time to be forced by the Texas state legislature to take American history courses. After all, most of them are science or business majors, and history is far from their chosen fields of interest. Rather than dismissing the study of history, they tell me that while engineers don't need to know history in order to build bridges, they need to know things like the Constitution in order to understand political and social controversies. Without saying so explicitly, they reflected the belief that some knowledge of history is a central element of responsible citizenship.

"Learning about, say, World War II," says one student, "makes you realize the dangers of monarchy and autocracy."

A female French major agrees. "Yeah, it's also knowing why we are how we are today. For instance, why do the French have such a bad opinion of Americans? It goes back to when they used to be one of the major world powers, and after World War II, they were no longer a world power; we had taken over. So if you look at history, you see why people have the attitudes they have now."

A serious-looking business major in a white T-shirt disagrees. "If I'm going to do business on the stock market, it doesn't matter if I know history." To my surprise, his peers point out that in a global economy, he had better know something of history and politics or he might misinterpret events and make bad investment decisions.

I ask if any particular interpretation of history is right. Several answer that history classes in high school presented them with one right answer, but in college they had come to realize that different people can come up with different interpretations. I wondered if they found their professors too liberal.

I am greeted with a sea of smiles. "You know," one replies, "that any teacher that you go to has their political beliefs. You can't say that a teacher can't have any political thoughts whatsoever. It may come across when they teach, but that's okay as long as they present both sides even when they don't agree with one."

I push them further. "There are people just down the road, state representatives, who say that you are being exposed to liberal views that undermine traditional American values, views that tell you not to celebrate traditional heroes like Columbus."

The room echoed with their snickers. "Come on!" a guy in a baseball cap reproaches me. "You need heroes when you're a child, but everybody has faults. Young people need heroes, but when you get older, that's when you start looking at the flaws. That doesn't make them less admirable, but everyone is flawed."

A tough-looking young man, who had earlier spoken passionately about the right to own a gun and who now complains that so many history books make villains out of great Americans, finishes with a grin. "I don't need professors or state legislatures telling me what to think. I can decide for myself."

Brands's class was yet another indication that students shape the goals and trajectories of their classes at least as much as their professors. And like Regina's class, these Texas A&M students evinced a marked disinclination to focus on details and a pronounced desire to trade opinions. But neither Regina Lark nor Bill Brands explicitly championed a particular interpretation of American history. The same cannot be said for a large lecture class at UC-Berkeley.

One autumn morning, more than five hundred students gather in a lecture hall in Berkeley. As Professor Pedro Noguera writes some notes on the board, announcements are made asking for volunteers to tutor local inner-city kids. Noguera, a trim, bearded man in his late thirties, clips on his microphone and steps forward. Young for a full professor, Noguera is also an activist in Berkeley and Oakland who is deeply involved in school-board politics. His reputation does indeed precede him. As he begins to speak, the room gradually falls silent.

Noguera exudes charisma. Speaking without notes, he conducts a seminar with hundreds of people. The course is on education, and it is part of Berkeley's controversial "American Cultures" requirement. At the beginning of the 1990s, Berkeley introduced a multicultural curriculum in response to student demands. Berkeley is a multicultural campus, and no one ethnic grouping comprises a majority. As of fall 1994, the freshman class was composed of 37 percent Asian Americans, 30.5 percent white, 17.1 percent Chicano/Latino American, 7.2 percent African American, and 1.5 percent Native American.[1] All students are required to take a course in American Cultures. In Texas, a student must take at least two terms of U.S. history. At Berkeley, a student must take at least one course that "approaches American majority and minority cultures as parts of an interacting, pluralistic whole." According to the mandate passed by the academic senate, "The goal is to teach Berkeley students about the United States in ways that take systematic account of the fact that a variety of cultural traditions and their interactions have shaped American experience." In order to avoid a "monocultural" approach, each American Cultures course must focus on the interaction of at least three major ethnic groups out of a possible five—white, Native American, Asian American, African American, and Latino.[2]

Course titles include "Lives of Struggle: Minorities in a Majority Culture," "Anthropology of American Minorities," "Marrying America: Marriage, Sexual Choices, and the Nation," "Introduction to Ethnic Studies," "Racial Inequality in America: A Comparative Historical Perspective," and Noguera's course, "Experiencing Education: Race and Ethnicity Inside Schools."

Since the Free Speech movement of the 1960s, Berkeley has been a radical campus, and in the 1980s, its radicalism was merged with multiculturalism to produce the American Cultures core. Students identify themselves by ethnic group, socialize with their ethnic cohorts, and take classes that focus on their ethnic culture and history. Yet they are also among the most career-minded college students in California. A high percentage were high school valedictorians; a majority of white and Asian students come from affluent families; and most graduates of all ethnicities go into careers in law, medicine, engineering, and other professions. While in college, however, radicalism is the theme; it is chic, like casual sex used to be. Once the students graduate, most of them glide naturally into the upper middle class.

Noguera lectures on the relationship between schooling and the capitalist economy. He talks about how school reinforces the socioeconomic inequalities in society and is a significant determinant of who will win and who will lose economically. He solicits student comments, and they add that schools play a role in socializing people to accept their economic state in life. School, the students say, is all about the class struggle between the haves and the have-nots. Those who have power use the school system to maintain their power. Noguera asks if anyone disagrees; no one speaks up.

He then points to the absence of a labor party in the United States. Isn't it odd, he asks, that there's no party that represents the working people? We have a system in the United States, he says, that leads the poor not to resent the rich but rather to resent being poor, and education gets young kids to accept things the way they are instead of encouraging them to challenge the status quo. He stresses that this isn't a conspiracy, but that almost makes it worse because people then come to see inequality as normal.

He starts to get warmed up. We live in a fragmented society, he says, where we don't see any responsibility for those less well off. We live in a winner-take-all system supported by the media and the schools. In school, we are constantly told what a great country this is. Slavery might have been bad, but look at what a magnificent country we built.

In school, we're taught how to interpret where we fit into society. He calls this the "hidden curriculum." Normal and appropriate ways of seeing things are inculcated indirectly, informally through dress codes and deference to authority.

Competitiveness is rewarded over cooperation, questioning the status quo is penalized, and knowing the answer is at a premium. A big part of what goes on in education, concludes Noguera, is what Paolo Freire calls "domestication,"[3] which creates an acceptance of domination. Teachers are held up as repositories of knowledge; students are blank slates. Thus, a power relationship is established in the classroom that lasts throughout life.

At the end of the lecture, I remained in my seat as five hundred multicolored students filed past me, talking about coffee and sex, laughing and teasing each other, men and women strutting into the midday sun. Noguera had walked a fine line between energetically expressing his perspective and indoctrination, and at times had crossed it completely. Student comments formed an amen chorus. With a thousand eyes focused on each student who stood to speak, it was ludicrous to think that anyone would get up and challenge what Noguera was saying. You could feel that a significant majority of the people in the room agreed with his analysis. It is hard enough to dissent in a small discussion group; it is almost impossible to do so in a large lecture. And Noguera himself stressed the power relationships in a classroom. He had the power. He rewarded students who spoke out to support his argument. Who in their right mind would challenge him? I left that day troubled by what had transpired.

Two days later, I return to his class and am astonished. This time Noguera discusses how the traditional goal of education in America was to provide a common culture. The fear was that if schools didn't do that, then there would be no glue holding American society together. "I said last time that the educational system sorts students, socializes us," he says. "But we are all individuals, not robots, and we have the capacity to change our environment and contest orthodoxies. Humans have the capacity to think critically; humans have agency."

He goes on. Most people accept the hidden curriculum because the American dream is real. The promise of wealth and success as the reward for hard work is genuine. If anyone doubts that it's genuine, just ask an immigrant. People come to this country, says Noguera, because it really does provide opportunities. There may be vast inequalities, but the potential for individual achievement is very real.

One day, Noguera seemed to be condemning the entire structure of American society and education as hegemonic tools to dominate the masses. The next day, he says, well, those tools can actually be the path to genuine success. One day, Abbie Hoffman would have been right at home; the next, William Buckley would have stood up and applauded. Unlike the two discussion classes in Canoga Park and Texas, Noguera's lectures were not even premised on a set of facts or narrative. He wanted his students to look at the link between education and American identity, and he wanted them to look through his eyes.

These are only three of tens of thousands of classes that convene each semester, but they are hardly anomalous. At Southern Methodist University in Dallas, where students deride the humanities as "Arts and Flowers," I sat in on a class where an explicitly lesbian English professor had her very Christian students read the play *Bent* about homosexuality in a Nazi prison camp. Several students felt that homosexuality was a sin but said that they took the class to be exposed to things they hadn't encountered in real life. At the State University of New York at Stony Brook, in an African American studies survey course with no white students, I watched the last half of the film *Glory*, about an all-black battalion in the Civil War. The professor, a former sixties activist, scolded his students when they condemned freed slaves for fighting for the white man. At Berkeley, in another American Cultures course, I witnessed the most direct, complicated discussion on race in America I had ever seen. The professor had ten students, each from different ethnic backgrounds, discuss Malcolm X. Opinions ranged from Malcolm as a saint to Malcolm as a violent misogynist. At the University of Texas at Austin, an English professor expressed his disdain for high-falutin' theory and told his students to stick to the text. The text in this case was T. S. Eliot's *The Wasteland*, and the professor took great delight in describing the sexual innuendos that weave their way through the poem.

The college classroom is a vibrant arena. Views are expressed there that would be incendiary in politics or in the media. But these opinions and perspectives are as varied and diverse as one would expect in a country of 250 million people. Free speech leads to strong disagreements, and college classes are one of the last safe arenas for the interplay of different perspectives. For all the furor over political correctness on campuses, a greater range of views gets expressed in unfettered language than in any other public realm of American society. Good teachers, and there are many of them, don't shy away from bringing their opinions to class, but they foster the capacity of their students to do the same.

Granted, for each provocative class, there are teachers who lecture and hardly make eye contact and students who fall asleep and refuse to say a thing. If someone wishes to drive home a point about the problems of higher education, it's easy to find a class that proves that point. It's also easy to find one that disproves it, and dozens that offer no clear statement either way.

From the above stories, however, it appears that in the tug-of-war between students and their professors, students often win and professors often concede. Professors may have the power to grade, but students have the power to enroll. Low enrollments spell trouble for a professor, and the power to grade is not uncontested by students. The Berkeley curriculum was not the brainchild of radical professors but the reaction of administrators toward student demands. In College Station, Texas, loyalty to the Second Amendment outweighs the qualms of the professor, while at Stony Brook, the alienation of young African Americans is stronger than the integrationist sentiments of their aging sixties teacher.

Furthermore, there is that tendency to revert to process, to spark interesting discussion at the expense of substantive discussion. After attending Regina Lark's class, or Pedro Noguera's, I wasn't optimistic that students had learned much beyond each other's point of view. That may be valuable, but it's not enough. Opinions without grounding in history or literature or anything other than personal experience may make for good arguments at a dinner party or good debates on television, but people do not need college just to help them express their opinions. And they don't need to go thousands of dollars into debt just to vent about the death penalty. They can do that by watching the news with friends and family.

The skills that college is supposed to teach require more thought, more discipline, and more rigor. Even though students often resist hard work, they tend to respect professors who insist that they do it, provided that these professors respect them. And students do not usually teach themselves. If the teacher doesn't insist that students apply themselves to what may be difficult reading and opaque concepts, then students will probably walk away having articulated their opinions and little else. In class after class, however, professors confront the passive or active refusal of their students to grapple with complex and difficult issues systematically.

What explains the inability of many professors to add substance to their students' passions? Why didn't Regina Lark even perceive that as lively as her class was, they were not learning certain valuable skills? Given their training, professors ought to understand the necessity of critical inquiry. The purported purpose of a graduate education and of the university in general is to ask hard questions and search for answers. These are the foundations of knowledge. However, professors are not trained how to teach, and increasingly, it is questionable how much critical thought graduate education actually inculcates. The problem is not the incompe-

tence of individual professors but the inadequacy of graduate education. Most professors spend their working hours as
teachers, yet they are trained to be scholars. It is time to turn
to these professors, and to begin at the beginning: graduate
school.

3

GRADUATE STUDENTS

Every year, about forty-five thousand men and women receive a piece of paper that confirms that they have earned the right to place "Dr." in front of their name. These forty-five thousand do not include medical doctors. These are the doctors of philosophy.[1] These are the professors of tomorrow and the graduate students of yesterday.

In theory, these newly minted Ph.D.'s will join the ranks of the half a million professors who teach college in the United States. In some fields, such as economics or engineering, a market for Ph.D.'s exists outside of the university. But for most fields in the humanities—for graduate students in English, history, philosophy, or ancient Assyriology—there is only one viable goal: a professorship at a university. And for most of these students, that is the sole reason for getting the Ph.D. in the first place.

Every spring, several hundred men and women gather at 8:00 A.M. in a quadrangle in Cambridge, Massachusetts. They are all wearing the same outfit. A long, crimson robe billows from each of their bodies, and on their heads is a felt four-cornered cap with a tassel. After a quick breakfast, these red-robed men and women, with friends, parents, and children in tow, begin to walk. Ten minutes later, a phalanx of crimson Erasmuses arrive in Harvard Yard and take their seats in the front rows. And then, as the ceremony commences, the president of Harvard University stands and welcomes them into the ancient fraternity of scholars.

The same scene, with different colors, is repeated throughout the country. The number of students earning Ph.D.'s has risen dramatically in the past decades, from nine thousand in 1958 to more than forty-five thousand in 1996. But graduate school for would-be Ph.D.'s is still confined to elite research universities. In 1958, sixty universities granted Ph.D.'s in English and history. By 1988, after explosive growth in undergraduate education, there were only 124 programs in history and 132 in English. The numbers are only slightly higher for nonhumanities programs, such as physics or mathematics.[2] Compared to the thousands of institutions offering a bachelor's or associate's degree, the world of graduate education is small, and the culture is homogenous. Graduate programs share values, aspirations, and goals.

Yet these values and goals no longer match the world that the preponderance of graduate students will occupy after they earn their degrees. Trained as research scholars, prepared for a life of minimal teaching with lifetime job security, new Ph.D.'s in the humanities soon discover that the real world of higher education today bears little resemblance to their expectations. With far more qualified applicants than available jobs, full-time employment as a professor, let alone tenure, is increasingly rare. Those who do get hired end up at state schools and community colleges with teaching responsibilities as extensive as any high school teacher. Equipped with highly specialized research skills, they find themselves at sea, to the detriment not just of their own psyches but of their students as well.

Universities are producing more Ph.D.'s each year. There were six hundred new history Ph.D.'s in 1988 and almost nine hundred in 1995. The numbers rose in almost every other major discipline.[3] Graduate school is more popular than ever, and it is harder to gain admission to the most select programs than to any undergraduate college. In fields such as psychology, hundreds of applicants apply to programs that admit fewer than ten. In fields such as history and English, the competition is only slightly less intense. Places like Harvard, Stanford, and Yale admit perhaps one in fifteen applicants.

Once admitted, a graduate student faces anywhere from four to ten years of school. Four years is uncommon, and in the humanities, almost unheard of. Seven years is typical. Seven years of study, and seven years of tuition. At public universities offering the Ph.D., tuition might total $50,000 in those seven years, while at private universities, the bill will easily exceed $100,000. And that is fees alone. Graduate students, in their mid to late twenties, often have families and children, and these need to be supported somehow. To be sure, the top students at the better schools will receive generous financial-aid packages, with tuition waivers and a $10,000 to $15,000 stipend. But many who are not subsidized will decide to use savings, parents, and federally subsidized loans in order to get through.

And for what? What is it that these thousands of neophyte scholars expect for these years of effort and the financial burden graduate school imposes? They know that in their first two or three years, they will be in the classroom, taking courses much as they took them in college. This time, however, the focus will be different. It is expected that they already know the basics of their field, and if they do not, they are expected to bring themselves up to speed, and quickly. Many first-year graduate students spend their time learning, really learning, what they studied superficially as undergraduates. When they were college students, that history course on Vietnam competed with play rehearsals, frat parties, a physics lab, and homecoming. Now that they are in graduate school, that history course is the focus. It is the reason for being.

In the humanities, students will often be required in their first year or two to become proficient in one or more foreign languages. The ancient community of scholars communicated in Latin, French, English, German, and Italian, and most fields retain a vestige of internationalism. The ability to read a foreign language is thought to be an essential component of scholarship, the mark of an educated person. Graduate students in American history cram the basic grammar of French and/or German so that they can pass an exam requiring them to translate a few paragraphs of said language into English. Dictionaries are permitted.

The crux of these first two years is the research seminar, capped by oral and written exams testing the Ph.D. candidate on his or her knowledge of the field. The seminars are designed to introduce the graduate student to the ways and methods of the scholar. Historians are shown how to evaluate primary documents. A medievalist might learn how to read manuscripts, and a scholar of Renaissance literature will be taught how to decipher various styles of handwriting.

At the same time, the grad student will ingest vast amounts of scholarship in order to learn how different questions have been answered by the fraternity of scholars. The historian of nineteenth-century America will read professors who argue that the Civil War was the result of the expansion of Northern industrial capitalism, and then read another who says that the root cause was the imperative to destroy slavery. The study of these debates in history is known as historiography, but every field has its equivalent.

The ins and outs of these debates, plus the sheer bulk of data that graduate students are expected to learn, form the basis of the first years of graduate school. At the end of this two or three years, the candidate is examined. This exam tests knowledge, often incredibly obscure knowledge. "What was the tenth of Woodrow Wilson's Fourteen Points?" "What was William Pitt the Younger's favorite book?" "What was the population of Buenos Aires in 1820?" "Compare the physical description of Humbert Humbert in *Lolita* with that of sexual predators in nineteenth-century English tabloids." "Explain the trends of capital formation in rural America in the decades after the American Revolution."

But after a few years of seminars and long reading lists, most Ph.D. students pass these exams. They were admitted to these select programs on the assumption that they had an aptitude for this type of study. On the whole, they did very well in their undergraduate classes, and those who manage to gain admission to a Ph.D. program usually prove capable of jumping through the hoops of these early years. The attrition comes later.

After three years of graduate school, therefore, the student has spent thousands of hours reading what scholars have written, debating what scholars have said, and learning how scholars have arrived at answers to questions that other scholars have posed. The next and last hoop is the dissertation. The dissertation is the capstone of the graduate career. The goal is for young scholars to produce a piece of original research, thereby adding their first brick to the edifice of scholarship. In the academic world today, the preference is to chose a topic that has escaped the notice of previous scholars.

Ideally, the topic should relate to the central concerns of the field at the moment. In the worlds of academic history, the current fashion is history from the bottom up rather than the traditional study of history from the top down or the center out. Thus, graduate students tend to pick topics that focus on the lives of ordinary people, of minorities, or of classes and individuals who until recently were invisible in most traditional historical narratives. One dissertation might study mill workers in early-nineteenth-century Lowell, Massachusetts, while another might look at prostitution in sixteenth-century Paris. Another will investigate peasant life in Ming China, while others will delve into burial rites amongst the Inca of Peru.

Other fields reflect this tendency to look at those on the margins of established society. One of the most popular fields of English is "subaltern studies," which is a branch of literature that focuses on the peoples who were the objects of colonial oppression. Novels of India, or Nigeria, and the fusion of traditional storytelling with European literary genres are the stock-in-trade for subaltern studies. Closely related to this subfield are the theories of the late French philosopher Michel Foucault and the current doyen of deconstructionism, Jacques Derrida—theories that stress the hidden relationships of power and oppression that characterize all literature, theories that taken to their logical end stress the constructedness of all reality. Reality is constructed by powerful elites, who set the rules of society, of history, of all texts and laws, in order to benefit themselves and keep the mass of humanity in a subservient position.

These theories are at the core of "postmodernism," and it is impossible to go to graduate school today without becoming aware of them. These ideas are so prevalent in academia that in many instances it is impossible not to begin seeing the world in postmodern terms. Dissertation after dissertation reflects the questions raised by postmodernism, questions that graduate students are introduced to in their first years as they read book after book on "the social construction of gender" or "the ideological constructs" that define our existence.

As many critics of higher education have noted, thirty years ago postmodernism did not exist. Graduate students and their professors studied familiar subjects such as Benjamin Franklin and William Shakespeare, and they studied familiar aspects of these individuals: "Romantic Love in Shakespeare's Plays" or "The Spirit of Discovery in Franklin's Early Years." Today, these critics complain, the subject is likely to be "Transgendering in Shakespeare's Plays" or "Homoeroticism in Franklin's Early Years."

However much "postmodernism" has changed the substance of academic research and scholarship, at a much deeper level graduate school and academia today are the same as they were thirty years ago, or even a century ago.[4] The topics may be different and the intellectual fashions may have changed, but at core it is as it ever was. The modern hierarchy of the university, with its credentialed professors and its core of preprofessional graduate students, developed in the middle of the nineteenth century. The evolution of this system in the United States owed something to the great English universities of Oxford and Cambridge but even more to the German academic model.[5]

The modern university is the child of the medieval monastery and the medieval guild, and deep in the recesses of the professoriate's identity is the model of the monk. The culture of academia, with its allegiance to an ideal of pure scholarship, formed over centuries continues to reflect attitudes that were prevalent among monks a thousand years ago.

The monk, who lived a life of austerity, meditation, in the company of other like-minded souls, solitary. The monk, who for years of the European "Dark Ages" preserved knowledge through painstaking transcription of ancient texts. It was a life marked by a deep and understandable distrust of the world outside. Monasteries were repositories not just of books but of rare objects and food as well. Roving bands of ragtag knights would just as soon sack a monastery as they would the castle of an adversary, and often sooner.[6]

Over time, some of these monks began to advance knowledge in addition to preserving it. The greatest theologian of the late Middle Ages was a Dominican monk, Saint Thomas Aquinas, whose thirteenth-century Latin treatises synthesized the philosophy of the Greeks with the theology of the Church fathers. As one of the greatest thinkers of his day, Aquinas became a professor at the University of Paris, where he debated his ideas with other seminal thinkers of his time.

The followers of Aquinas, known as Thomists, were contested by a loose association of monks known as the Scholastics, many of whom adhered to the wisdom of Aristotle and St. Augustine. One of the main contentions of the Scholastics was that knowledge must be based on empirical observation except knowledge of God, which Scholastics asserted could only come from faith. Though Aquinas disagreed with many Scholastic teachings, he too stressed the need for philosophy and knowledge to be grounded in careful, meticulous observation of the material world.

In the most general sense, the Thomists and the Scholastics in turn provided the intellectual foundations of the Renaissance and of centuries of thought that led to the championing of empiricism and science over religion and revelation as the keys to knowledge. But the Thomists and the Scholastics never really disappeared, and their descendants can be found in the university today.

The modern university that emerged in Germany in the nineteenth century placed the community of scholars at the center of intellectual life. Like the medieval monastery, the German university was inward looking, a place where professors studied and wrote, quietly, with a few select students. These professors, men such as Georg Friedrich Hegel and Leopold von Ranke, developed philosophies of knowledge that tried to explain history and the reason for being in material rather than religious terms. They examined the world and derived theories. These "scholars" were the heirs to the legacy of the Scholastics.

Scholars created codes of conduct for each other, the dos and don'ts of the scholarly life. Monkish orders were based on "rules" set down by the founder of the order. So too the modern university had rules, rules that in the nineteenth century stressed the empirical bases of knowledge on the one hand and the danger that the political and social world posed for scholarship on the other. The sense that the world outside the walls of the monastery was an ever-present threat to what went on inside made its way into the psyche of the modern university. For knowledge to be pure, it had to be unencumbered by utility. For knowledge to be reliable, it had to rest on neutral, empirical observation. Any other foundation was suspect.

The other parent of the modern community of scholars is the medieval guild. A medieval *universitas* was a guild or corporation composed of people engaged in the same occupation. Coppersmiths were one universitas, tailors another, masons yet another and perhaps the most famous, and so on for each profession. Guilds determined what was and wasn't acceptable business practice, and they acted as early interest groups presenting the grievances of their members to local rulers.

Membership in a guild was a necessary prerequisite to plying a trade, and membership could be gained by birth and by apprenticeship. Apprentices, usually young boys, were taken on and given the most menial tasks, but by watching and listening, they would in time begin to learn the skills they would need to practice the craft themselves. They were ill housed, badly fed, shoddily clad, and barely paid, but that was a reasonable price for learning skills that in time would allow them to earn a livelihood, support a family, and enjoy a place and even prestige in society.

By the late nineteenth century, the community of scholars had begun to separate knowledge into the modern disciplines: literature, classics, history, geography, anthropology, psychology. In the United States, these disciplines were given cohesion by professional organizations, such as the Modern Language Association (1883), the American Historical Association (1884), the American Philosophical Association, the American Political Science Association, and many others.[7]

In 1915, led by the pragmatic philosopher John Dewey, the American Association of University Professors was founded, "to facilitate a more effective cooperation among the members of the profession in the discharge of their special responsibilities as custodians of the interests of higher education and research in America . . . and to maintain and advance the standards and ideals of the profession."[8] Composed entirely of professors, the AAUP and the professional organizations helped determine the rules of the professoriate. The AAUP articulated the concept that professors should have job security, free from the ebbs and flows of the marketplace on the one hand and the intellectual caprice of society on the other. Without tenure, said the AAUP, there could be no intellectual freedom, and without intellectual freedom, knowledge would suffer.

The professional organizations were devoted almost entirely to research. The ethos of the scholar was scholarship, and teaching was not a central part of that ethos. In order to keep the flames of scholarship alive, however, new scholars had to be produced, or the flame would die. While teaching undergraduate students was seen as a secondary activity, nurturing young scholars was a priority. The professional organizations helped set the standards for training scholars. They helped define what the doctorate of philosophy should entail, and they codified what was expected of the community. Like medieval guilds, they set guidelines for apprentices, who in time became known as graduate students.

Many contemporary academics don't realize that the university of today is a legacy of the monasteries and guilds of old, and many would dispute that there is any resemblance. But while today's universities are vastly more complex and bureaucratic places, with undergraduate cultures and sports complexes that bear little relation to Thomas Aquinas, today's scholars resemble the monks and Scholastics of a thousand years ago more than they might like to think.

Graduate school is the crucible of young scholars, and it is there that they learn values that have their roots deep in the recesses of Western history. In graduate school, the student is an apprentice, and the hierarchy is clear. At the top are the full professors, the dons of the modern university. Graduate students approach these professors with respect, reverence, occasional awe, often with a healthy sprinkling of resentment. Each grad student has a mentor, an advisor who oversees the work of the student and who has the power to grant or withhold rewards as petty as travel money for research and as significant as the Ph.D. itself. Graduate students look to their advisors for intellectual guidance and sustenance, for criticism and advice, and for all sorts of formal and informal professional advancement. They ask their advisors for letters of recommendation that can make the difference in winning a prestigious fellowship or landing a coveted job.[9] And they often end up looking to their professors not just for guidance but for inspiration.

After passing their exams, graduate students embark on the dissertation, yet they often have no idea what they will research. The process of searching for a dissertation topic can take months or years, and grad students often turn to their advisors in despair and ask for help. Professors oblige by giving their students a topic, a topic that is probably related to the professor's own research and that will address questions that said professor has been unable to answer. Graduate students, as good apprentices, then do years of work that enhances the work of their sponsor, their mentor. In return, they hope to be rewarded with membership in the guild. They hope to be welcomed, one sunny spring day, into the ancient fraternity of scholars.

It is a romantic picture: graduate school, the first step on a sacred path. In one respect, graduate school is isolated from the dislocations of modern industrial society. You spend hours in a library, or at home, reading, thinking, and writing. You go to seminars several times a week and talk in highly abstract terms, inaccessible to the uninitiated, unintelligible to those outside of your guild. You spend untold hours in front of a computer screen, trying to tease from thousands of pages of notes some meaningful prose, some cogent theory, some probing analysis that will set you apart from your peers. And you look always to your mentors, whose goodwill you depend on and without whose support you will never advance.

Graduate school embodies the values of Scholasticism, of empiricism, of knowledge and research for the sake of knowledge and research. It inculcates the idea of apprenticeship, with the promise of eventual membership in the guild. It encourages students to withdraw from society and asks them to exchange the workaday life of most Americans for the rarefied world of scholarship.[10]

But there's a problem. Few graduate students can afford to withdraw from the workaday world. Most of them must work, and hard, and most recognize that the promise of guild membership in the form of a job is a rapidly dwindling prospect. And the ideal of pure scholarship, however appealing to monks of the Dark Ages and Germans of the nineteenth century, is less easy to reconcile with the fluctuating landscape of higher education today than it was at any point in the past. Graduate school promises a refuge from the buffeting disruptions of material society. Students enter the library ready to plunge into the accumulated knowledge of scholarship. Then they come out into the bright sun, furiously blinking and unable to adjust to the world before them.

The actual experience of graduate school rarely bears more than passing resemblance to the image of graduate school. In fact, this dissimilarity is often so great that many students become thoroughly disillusioned and quit. Among those who stay, the levels of cynicism and bitterness are astounding.

While it was once common for the brightest undergraduates to enter the select Ph.D. programs, graduate school is increasingly filled with the diverse, nontraditional students that comprise a significant portion of the undergraduate community. "I entered the graduate department of history at Tulane University with a B.A. from the University of Texas at Arlington," says Stan. "I was a nontraditional student, middle-aged, coming from a less than prestigious undergraduate program. Until 1987, I was a skilled technician who maintained computerized machine tools and robots in an industrial setting. I had little in common with my coworkers." Stan found that his interests in art and history were nurtured by his professors at Arlington, and he was urged to pursue a career as an academic. Tulane offered him a fellowship and a tuition waiver, and he enrolled with a natural mix of anxiety and hope.

"Less than a month after my arrival, ominous signs made me doubt the wisdom of my choice. The primary problem was my proposed field of study. My advisor not only vetoed my proposal but acted as if he was unaware of my acceptance into the Tulane program." When he confronted the head of the department, the chairman told him that since his Graduate Record

Exam scores had been so high, the admissions committee might not have bothered to read his proposed course of study.

"I was both mystified and horrified," Stan continued. "After all, I had made both a material and an emotional commitment by entering Tulane's graduate school. Moving to New Orleans had been costly, and I had left a reasonable financial situation at home. Moreover, I had staked a good deal of self-esteem on successful completion of a Ph.D. program. Family and friends were rooting for me. Letting them down would have been embarrassing.

"I decided to make myself acceptable to Tulane's history department and my advisor, regardless of cost. It was at this point that the Ph.D. became an end in itself rather than a means toward a higher goal. The topics that genuinely interested me moved to the back burner, presumably to be taken up again after the Ph.D. granted me a license to think. I now placed a premium on pleasing an advisor whose interests and views differed fundamentally from mine. Such a relationship meant that I would follow his whims rather than a coherent plan of study. During my nearly five-year Tulane experience, I always was aware of my intellectual loss. Unfortunately, the same cannot be said about my self-respect. Getting along in Tulane's graduate program is largely an exercise in humiliation. In front of class, one professor told me that as a graduate student, I was not entitled to opinions. My advisor found my offbeat appearance unacceptable. To gain his approval, I quickly cut my long hair and spent $300 on a new wardrobe."

Stan did well in his program, routinely earning A minuses, although he soon realized that almost all graduate students get B pluses at the very least. "No department wants to make a bad showing by flunking out one of its funded students. This is especially true when the university is facing financial difficulties, and all departments are under close scrutiny. It's imperative that each department present a rosy picture of its graduate program lest it lose scholarships to other departments. It is easy to see that a student could pass through years of graduate courses, hold an excellent grade-point average, and still not possess a fundamental knowledge of the field. After all, professors normally fail to provide basic instruction in their field, and students are not held accountable because grades are kept artificially high."

Stan's disenchantment is palpable. In relation to others in his position, he is both more bitter and perhaps less mature. But almost anyone who has been through graduate school can relate to his experience. It is often the case that advisors are disengaged and condescending. The hierarchy of academia has a tendency to infantilize even the brightest of graduate students, no matter what their age. Relationships between bosses and subordinates in the commercial workplace can be fraught with tension, and stories abound of petty, abusive bosses who make the lives of those under them miserable. Advisors, however, are not answerable to anyone except their own conscience and their sense of fealty toward what the community of scholars suggests their behavior ought to be.

Many professors take their obligations toward graduate students extremely seriously. After all, without graduate students, the profession would eventually wither and die, and scholars feel the imperative to replicate themselves no less than other professionals. Some professors, however, abuse their power and make it clear to their graduate students that they hold the keys to success. Hence, pleasing one's advisor becomes an obsession for many graduate students at the expense of pursuing intellectual questions. There is a world of difference between pleasing one's advisor and posing challenging new questions. Pleasing an advisor frequently means embracing his or her intellectual and political perspective. That is conformity, and it often results in derivative work that copies in jargon and method the work of the advisor. An apprentice in a medieval guild was expected to copy the work of the master. Art historians talk of the "school of Raphael" or the "school of Titian" to identify paintings not by the master painter but done in the same style by disciples of the master. There could, in theory, be merit to graduate students copying the methods of their mentors, but more often than not, the copy is but a pale reflection of the original.

This has been an intellectual weakness of graduate school since its inception. Though today's undergraduates feel free to challenge the authority of their professors, graduate students rarely feel free to do so with their advisors. That is because the power of advisors to penalize their grad students for deviant thought is far greater than the capacity of teachers to penalize their undergraduates.

Fear pervades graduate school. Students often choose dissertation topics based not on the merits of the question or on the social importance of the problem but on what the community of scholars will accept and reward. The first line of that community is the advisor, but the ethos of the profession as a whole must also be considered. Again, graduate students have always tried to please their mentors and do work that satisfies the field, but there used to be some assurance that a Ph.D. from an elite school meant entry into the guild. That meant that there were jobs, and the implicit formula was that if you do as you're told and learn the scholarly trade, then you'll get a job and have a long and fruitful career.

That system no longer works. The jobs aren't there, and the subjects of dissertations are so arcane and field-specific that graduate students lose touch with anything except their small piece of intellectual turf. Each year, the number of new Ph.D.'s outstrips the number of jobs; given that many Ph.D.'s will spend several years looking for a full-time assistant professorship, each year the backlog grows and adds to the glut of qualified applicants. Hard numbers are difficult to come by. Several years ago, Harvard University reported that job prospects for its Ph.D.'s were extremely grim. Then a new study was commissioned, and the results improved. Harvard reported that within three years of completing their degrees, 71 percent of Ph.D.'s in the social sciences had found jobs in academia, 51 percent in the natural sciences, and 81 percent in the humanities.[11] However, many of these "jobs" are one-year positions, or "non–tenure track" contracts for three years or less. These rosy numbers might be expected from one of the premier graduate schools in the country, but even for those who spend *three years* looking for a job, there is still a 19-percent unemployment rate for Harvard humanities graduates, a 29-percent rate for social sciences such as history, and nearly 50 percent for natural sciences. Most of these do find nonacademic jobs, but even at Harvard, many Ph.D. students do not obtain jobs in the field for which they were trained.

Overall, the statistics point to severe employment problems, and voluminous anecdotal evidence underscores just how depressed the job market is.[12] The National Research Council estimates that 923 people received Ph.D.'s in English in 1994, an increase of 20 percent from ten years before. Of those, barely 40 percent gained tenure-track full-time jobs.[13] In history, the number of new Ph.D.'s increased by more than 35 percent in the 1990s, and it is estimated that one-third of them will *never* find full-time employment.[14]

The job crisis of academia in general and the humanities in particular began in the 1970s. Until then, the number of Ph.D.'s awarded lagged behind the number of new faculty appointments.[15] But as college enrollments stabilized with the tail end of the baby boomers, new Ph.D.'s rolled off graduate-school assembly lines and discovered that there were far fewer jobs than 1960s college enrollments had indicated there would be. Because the community-college system was relatively small in the 1970s, the job crisis was actually worse then than it is now. But while community colleges mean that there are more jobs today, many of these are part-time, and people such as Regina Lark teach as adjuncts.[16] Even where these are full-time, they are primarily teaching jobs, and graduate school does not train teachers. Graduate school trains scholars.

The skewed supply-and-demand employment curve in higher education has consequences beyond graduate school, and we will come to these shortly. The economy of higher education is only dimly understood by most academics, and the social and intellectual consequences of the job market of the last three decades are equally unclear. Many professors and graduate students adopt a fatalistic attitude, saying "What can we do about it?" For many graduate students, who have invested years of effort and money, finishing the Ph.D. is the only viable option, and the hope that somehow you will be the one to get the job is the only thing that keeps you going. One Harvard French professor explained that while the job market demoralizes graduate students, "People think, I'll be the lucky one, and that allows them to keep working."[17]

Economic anxiety and fear beset many Americans these days, of course, and graduate students may partly be experiencing their own version of a much larger social phenomenon. And while it may not be optimal that graduate students live lives marked by internal anxiety and by the external pettiness of advisors, it would hardly seem to rank as a social problem of the first order. Yet, the job crunch has intellectual and social consequences that should concern both the guild and the society at large. Because of the pressure to get a job and the odds against landing one, graduate students are becoming ever more likely to conform to the orthodoxies of their field and ever less likely to be able to communicate with the world outside of the academy. That has negative effects on undergraduates and on the scholarly community, and it makes it nearly impossible for academics to do work that bears on social and political issues of the day.

If you survey dissertation topics in any humanities field, it's hard not to be struck by the conformity of the topics. There is a lemminglike quality to the intellectual product that graduate students produce. The overwhelming majority of American history doctoral studies today are on social history and "new" history, with emphasis on postmodernism and all of its many cousins. Conservative critics of the academy have noted this trend and pointed to it as proof that academics are radicals bent on overturning traditional American values. Unfortunately, these critics have misinterpreted the trend. On the whole, it is not the result of radical ideology but rather the inevitable product of the intellectual orthodoxies that academic guilds promote.

At Memphis State University, dissertation topics ranged from "19th-Century Prostitution in Memphis" to "Rock 'n' Roll, and Elvis Presley: Southern Youth in Dissent, 1948–1963." At the University of Michigan at Ann Arbor, there is "Constructing Urban Space and Community Identity in South Chicago, 1892–1929," "Southern Attitudes toward Immigration, 1820–1924," "The Consumer Experience in Post-Revolutionary Philadelphia: A Social History of Cultural Change." At Temple, we have "Democratic Assassins: Spousal Homicide in America, 1830–1920"; at Cornell, "Newspapers, Myths, and Patty Hearst: Constructing Culture the Hearst Way, 1892–1992"; at the University of Arkansas, "Violet Blair and Albert Janin: A Study of a 19th-Century Marriage."

These topics are representative of the trends in the history profession. For each of these, there are a dozen others in a

similar vein, while for a dozen of these, there may be one on
Eisenhower and the space program, William Howard Taft
and the Progressive movement, JFK and the New Frontier.
The shift away from high politics, or "great man" history, is
particularly evident in the subject of papers at the AHA. At
the 1950 American Historical Association conference, topics
on high politics predominated. One panel was "The Historian and the Federal Government: Research and Publication
Opportunities." There were sessions on FDR and World War
II, as well as discussions on military history, Alexander
Hamilton, and U.S. foreign policy in the early twentieth century. The closest things to social history were a panel on slavery and a panel on agriculture.

Jump twenty years to 1970, and out of ninety-nine panels,
the majority were on issues such as feminism, "History from
a Black Perspective," "Women's Experience in History,"
"Civil Rights and the Negro Farmer," "The Social History of
Colonial Latin America," "The New Deal and the New Left,"
and "The Process of Acculturation: The Black and the Jew."
There were still a good number of talks on traditional history, but the focus had shifted. At the 1996 conference, out
of 140 panels, the index listed more than 80 on social, race,
gender, family, and gay/lesbian history.

The mission statement of UCLA's history department,
printed in the course catalog and sent to all prospective applicants, says: "Its main emphasis is on the many aspects of
social history, but intellectual, cultural, and political history
are strongly represented." At UCLA the course list is dominated by Chicano history, history of the family, history of im-

migrants, North American Indian history, the social history of American women, African American history. Asked why UCLA has decided to focus on the areas it does, Joyce Appleby, one of the most respected historians in the United States today and past president of the American Historical Association, explained to me that "the social history of women, of the enslaved, the oppressed had been neglected in the past. In addition, many of the undergraduates and graduates at UCLA are Chicano, or African American, or women, or people whose roots are very different than the Boston Brahmins who used to dominate the profession. These students want to understand their own roots."

UCLA is not alone. At neighboring UC-Riverside, out of eleven historians teaching U.S. history, not one does political history. One person focuses on economics, another on science, several on various aspects of social and African American history, but no one writes on high politics or foreign policy. At Texas Tech, not exactly a hotbed of radicalism, the courses listed are studies in: nineteenth-century U.S. history, with emphasis on journals; recent U.S. history; Texas history; Southern history; frontier history; American agriculture; rural American history; Native American history; legal and constitutional history; U.S. diplomatic history; American economic history; American environmental history; African American history; Mexican American history. At Cornell, there are twelve professors of Native American history, Asian American history, African American history, and various aspects of social history, but only three on political history. At the University of Alabama, the numbers are ten to three; at

Northwestern, nine to three, with the nine focusing on lesbian-gay history, cultural anthropology and colonial history, and economic history.

In English departments, there is a similar move away from the classical literature familiar to students of the 1940s and 1950s.

The specific research topics notwithstanding, anyone familiar with graduate students would be hard-pressed to describe them as flaming radicals. Graduate students see the current trend. They see the absolute scarcity of jobs, and they see what type of work is rewarded, with jobs and publications, and what type is not. Understandably, they try to choose a dissertation topic that suits the current sensibility of their mentors and of the field as a whole. If few professors in history are focusing on traditional politics, then few graduate students will study traditional politics. If gender is "in," then gender will be the subject of dissertations.

Thirty years ago, gender wasn't "in." Nor was race or pop culture. In the 1950s and early 1960s, topics were as skewed toward high politics, military history, and "great men" as they are today toward race, gender, and class. Young graduate students in these years chafed at the narrowness of acceptable questions, and as all young generations tend to, they tried to expand the envelope. Combine that with the heady days of 1960s activism, and you get the now familiar race/gender/class triumvirate in the humanities.

In one sense, this triumvirate ought to have widespread appeal outside the university. Americans of all stripes are interested in and troubled by relations between the sexes, among the classes, and across racial lines. Research that focuses on different aspects of these relationships could appeal to broad audiences, from curious undergraduates to equally concerned senior citizens. But academic jargon and intensely complex argumentation make contemporary academic work inaccessible to the general public. The only audience for the papers at the AHA and for the hundreds of dissertations is the community of scholars, and when professors or graduate students attempt to broaden the audience and simplify the questions, they are frequently greeted with criticism if not outright condescension.

Certain intellectual fashions that fall under the rubric of postmodernism have dominated the humanities for a couple of decades, and given the life cycle of orthodoxies, it would seem high time for a younger generation to begin questioning its basic premises. In the 1960s, younger scholars questioned the then current traditions of "great man" history and high literature. But today, if you write something outside the academic mainstream, you will likely alienate established scholars, scholars who sit on hiring committees and determine who gets those precious few entry-level jobs. Write something that provides an intelligent variation on a familiar theme, and your chances are far better.

Some dispute that the nature of academic orthodoxies combined with a restricted job market leads to intellectual timidity on the part of graduate students. Professor Jim Sidbury of UT-Austin believes that only those graduate students who do something innovative have a shot at a job. There's so much that is derivative, he says, that the few that aren't stand out and are rewarded.[18]

Perhaps, but an added factor suggests otherwise. Many of today's graduate students entered grad school not because they hoped to boldly go where no one has gone before but because the uncertain economic climate in the United States made graduate school seem like a safe haven in an otherwise tumultuous commercial job market. Time and again, professors remark on the discomfort their grad students feel with the marketplace, not because they are in any way anticapitalist but because stories of downsizing, stagnant wages, and economic turmoil make graduate school seem like Circe's island.

There's no hard evidence that graduate students as a whole are less comfortable than any other group with the cutthroat quality of the American job market at the close of the millennium. But that sense is palpably there. It is probably true that graduate students have always tended to follow the lead of the professors above them. In early periods, however, academic orthodoxies did not entail the types of theory and jargon that characterize current scholarship. As a result of these new orthodoxies, graduate students pursue research topics that remove them from the larger culture.

People outside the university rarely care, and even more rarely can understand, what academics are talking about. Yet people do care about similar issues. There are heated social and political debates over gun control, and opponents and proponents draw on the Constitution and moments of American history to support their side of the debate. Yet when graduate students and professors deal with the same issue, the writing and the research are likely to have little relevance to those public debates because the intellectual frameworks and the language of academia make the work unintelligible and hence largely unintelligible to the larger public.[19]

In one respect, however, graduate students are increasingly thrust into contact with that public—as teachers. It used to be that graduate school was separate from and prior to the next stage of the academic career. Graduate students attended seminars, read books, researched a dissertation topic, and wrote. Over the past decades, however, graduate students have taken on an ever increasing portion of undergraduate teaching. At the same time that they are burrowing into academic minutiae, they are being asked to assume responsibilities once reserved solely for professors.

Regina Lark held dual identities as both graduate student and teacher, and she is far from alone. Not only must grad students find adjunct teaching positions to supplement their income, but they are expected as part of their degree to serve as teaching assistants for lecture courses taught by their professors. At the large public and private universities that have graduate programs, a significant portion of undergraduate teaching is done by graduate students. In English departments, graduate students teach composition, and in history they teach surveys. In addition, teaching assistants do most of the grading. It is one of the ironies of a Harvard or Yale education, for example, that while these schools sell themselves on their all-star faculty, and while students will be able to go and listen to these all-stars speak, undergraduate grades are determined by graduate students.

For teaching a survey course, leading a discussion section, and grading, teaching assistants are fortunate if they can earn more than $10,000 to $12,000 a year. Pay varies from place to place, but the range tends to be from a low of $1,000 per course to a high of over $3,000. Compare that to a starting salary of about $40,000 a year for an assistant professor in the humanities. Many of these graduate students are in their thirties, have families and children, and are expected first and foremost to be working toward the completion of their dissertation. But they need to teach two to four sections a term in order to pay their bills. Teaching assistantships are the primary form of financial aid for graduate students, and departments depend on these low-paid TAs to do the requisite undergraduate grading and introductory teaching that professors are not inclined to do.

As undergraduate enrollments mushroom at state schools, graduate students take on larger teaching burdens, while professors try to maintain or even lessen their own teaching responsibilities to give them more time for research. Graduate students, however, are rarely prepared to teach. Their first years of graduate school introduce them to scholarship, and the dissertation draws them deeply into the realm of academic knowledge. Teaching simply isn't part of the graduate student mind-set and it isn't usually part of their training. It is, however, a central part of what universities do.[20]

In recent years, graduate students have begun to demand that universities treat them as workers and not simply as students. TAs are not only low paid; they also aren't given any benefits such as health insurance or Social Security. Their labor is an integral part of large universities, yet they are treated as students, both financially and professionally. At places such as Yale, the University of Illinois at Urbana-Champaign, or UCLA, graduate students perform some of the same functions as professors, and undergraduates pay the same tuition to be taught by graduate students as they do to be taught by professors.

In response, graduate students at a number of universities have tried to unionize, or at least organize themselves to negotiate collectively with university administrators. In the fall of 1995, graduate students at Yale went on strike to protest their working conditions and pay.[21] In 1996, graduate students at UCLA briefly went on strike for similar reasons, and sympathy strikes took place at Berkeley, UC-Santa Barbara, and UC-San Diego. Administrators responded angrily. It isn't in the university's financial interest to pay teaching assistants more than they are currently paid, and the administrations of these schools argued that TAs are not workers but rather students whose teaching responsibilities are part of their education.[22]

Professors at Yale were, for the most part, solidly against graduate-student unionization efforts. They were outraged that their students would go on strike and interpreted the action as a personal betrayal. Many of these professors had written books exposing the ill treatment of workers in capitalist systems of the past, and many made careers studying the "literature of the oppressed." Yet their response to striking graduate students was swift and unequivocally hostile.[23] Professor Peter Brooks told the *New York Times* that in his view, graduate students "really are among the blessed of the earth . . . so I sometimes feel annoyed at them for seeing themselves as exploited."

In late 1996, the National Labor Relations Board recognized the right of graduate students to bargain collectively, and it announced that it would consider taking action against universities that attempted to infringe on that right. But the structure of graduate school, with its roots deep in the past and its guildlike hierarchies, has little room for graduate-student unions collectively negotiating for their "workers." Professors wish to see graduate students as apprentices or junior colleagues, not as coworkers, and administrators are determined to retain this cheap, educated labor pool.

Unless state legislators are willing to allocate more money to fund pay increases for teaching assistants, or students are willing to pay higher tuition, or professors accept salary cuts, it is hard to see where the money would come from to raise the salaries of graduate assistants. Departments could also admit fewer graduate students and thereby offer them more financial aid or more teaching money, but in many places, enrollments are actually growing.

Faced with stiff teaching loads and a depressing job market, many graduate students put off completing their dissertations, and many drop out altogether. Attrition rates are hard to come by, as most departments do not wish to keep a record of their failures.[24] Meanwhile, those who do grind toward the finish seek the haven of a full-time assistant professorship. Those who do land a job at a college or university will then be at the bottom of a ladder that will culminate in tenure, if all goes as planned. Those who do not will float on the margins of academia, as adjuncts, visiting lecturers, and one-year replacements.

Almost all graduate students aspire to become tenured professors, but a large portion will fall short of that goal. Graduate school trains students to become scholars, though many will be asked instead to be remedial instructors of those millions of new undergraduates. One innovative program at New York City's Hunter College prepares new Ph.D.'s for careers teaching in prisons.[25] Most graduate students can expect to head in one of two directions—into the ranks of the tenured professoriate or into an academic underworld of minimal wages, little respect, and no security. The underworld is growing, while the safe havens of tenure are beginning to disappear.

Many professors claim that a doctoral education should not be based on the availability of jobs or sufficient financial aid. "Why are graduate schools somehow morally responsible for ensuring that graduates get the jobs of their choice?" asked one professor. In department after department, the same refrain echoes. Graduate education is a noble calling, offering students "the joys of the life of the mind."[26] According to these professors, whether or not jobs are available for these students is, therefore, irrelevant. Some schools have begun to reconsider this blithe refusal to acknowledge that graduate education has changed, as have the quality and quantity of jobs.[27] Some departments are decreasing the size of their programs to reflect the oversupply. But more often than not, professors and administrators prattle on about "the joys of the life of the mind" while fiddling with the careers of their graduate students with all of the care and morality of Nero in Rome.

The academic profession is still predicated on an organic progression from graduate school to assistant professorship

to tenure. That is what academics believe is natural, just as most Americans have some vague notion that life should consist of high school in the suburbs, college, a job, a marriage, and children in a two-parent family living in a house with a white picket fence. Those graduate students who get hired as tenure-track assistant professors find themselves on the next rung of the academic ladder, relieved to have made it to the next stage and ready to begin their new lives as junior members of the guild.

4

THE
PROFESSORS

Let's look for a moment at the life of our average professor of the humanities. Our professor, let's call him Professor Smith, teaches at State University. He is forty-five years old, white, and male. He earns between $50,000 and $60,000 annually. He has a moderately sized office with one window, an overhead light, a desk lamp, and a computer. His office is lined with books and file cabinets, giving a slightly musty feel to an otherwise modern space. The state campus that employs him has probably been built in the last thirty years. The buildings are concrete blocks, only slightly more inviting than housing projects of the same period. If our professor is fortunate, he will work at one of the more richly endowed private schools and be able to gaze out his window onto a manicured quadrangle with older brick buildings and stately trees.

Our professor teaches four to six courses a year, and he spends between six and twelve hours a week in class during the thirteen-week semesters each fall and spring. Most of those courses are lecture courses; several are introductory lectures, while the rest are for more advanced students. If his state school has graduate students, he will also teach a graduate seminar in which he will supervise readings and discussions that introduce the grad students to the methodologies of the field. For his lecture courses, our professor will spend anywhere from ten to twenty hours a week preparing and grading. If it's a course he has taught before, as it very likely is, the preparation time is less, but there is always grading. In the largest lecture courses, some of that grading will be done by our professor's teaching assistants.

In addition to teaching, Professor Smith will sit in his office and meet with students. They will come in to discuss their grades, their interests, their disagreements with their grades, their papers, their future, and their problems. Our professor will listen politely, and in some cases he may take a personal interest. He will write recommendation letters, take his favorite students out for coffee or a meal, and hope that they keep in touch after they graduate.

Our professor will also spend many hours each week during term on administrative matters. There are departmental committees to oversee hiring, to determine course requirements for undergraduate majors, and to set departmental budgets. There are also university committees on affirmative action, student discipline, student housing, and fund-raising and search committees for deans and other administrators. These meetings and the preparation for them consume many hours of our professor's week.

In the hours that remain, Professor Smith will attend to the work he cares most about, his research. He will trundle over to the library during the winter and pore through the stacks. He will sit and read old manuscripts, new books, and recent journals. He will take notes, jot down paragraphs, doodle in the margins of his note cards, play a game of solitaire on his laptop. And all the while, his mind will be spinning, thinking of the various arguments or observations that he might make, contemplating the objections his colleagues might raise, wondering how he might hone the argument until it is unassailable. Or he will think of how it might come together in the conference paper he's scheduled to deliver later that month, and he will hope that the more eminent members of the field will be there.

During the thirty weeks of the year that our professor teaches, he will feel overwhelmed and pressured. There never seems to be enough time to sit down and write, but it's been three years since he's published anything, and the dean has elected not to raise his pay as a result. His friends constantly ask him what he's working on, and he feels hard-pressed to answer. He has this idea he's been kicking around for a few years, and he'd really like to carve out a few months and focus on it, but one thing leads to another during the term, and before he knows it, another three months have passed.

The month between fall and spring terms is a welcome break, but with Christmas and family events, he doesn't get much more done. His annual conference meets just after New Year's, and while there, he has a chance to catch up on what other professors and their graduate students are doing in his field. He also runs into old friends, who ask him what he's working on.

After the spring term, he's really looking forward to a summer of research. Our professor has managed to read a few dozen books, and he's convinced that the leading scholars in his field have missed some critical interpretive angle. He's managed to get the chair of the department to give him some research money, and he hopes that the summer will prove fruitful. That fall, with his work half finished, he returns to class. Maybe he'll finish that year, but if not, he has an entire term off that spring. It's his sabbatical, and he looks forward to productive months of research.

Our professor lives in a world marked by the academic calendar, a world whose priorities are determined by the guild. Those priorities are his priorities. Rarely is he thinking of an audience beyond scholars in his field. His professional reputation is determined by them, and his career rides on that reputation. Our professor is the academic man in the gray flannel suit.

But there are others in the university who see themselves differently. They see the university as a base that will allow them to be active in society. Many of these fall on the left of the political spectrum and identify themselves as children of 1960s activism. You would think that these activists would transcend the boundaries of their profession and of the guild, but they rarely do. Professor Smith is the product of a culture that places the guild at the center of a professor's life. It is a testament to the strength of this guild that even the most radical, up-the-establishment firebrand finds that radicalism neatly contained.

The University of Texas at Austin sits quietly on a hill, its white stone buildings and trimmed lawns surmounted by a tall tower. In that tower sits the president of the university, and if he cranes his neck out of the window and looks south, he can see another tall tower, the cupola of the Texas statehouse.

Over the decades, the legislators in the statehouse have fulminated against the professors in the buildings up the street. These legislators, hailing from towns like Corpus Christi and Lubbock, from one-horse towns that dot the landscape of east Texas and the ranches that occupy thousands of acres in west Texas, have never much cared for those liberals at the university, and the fact that the state pays the salaries of those professors is taken by many legislators as a license to dictate who can teach and what can be taught.

Just to the east of the university tower is Garrison Hall, which houses the UT-Austin history department. The top floor of Garrison is a converted attic space, with a sloped roof and low ceilings. This space was converted some years ago to offices—small cubbies, actually. There are no windows, just fluorescent light, computers, and bookshelves for the assistant professors. In one of these sits Neil Foley, recently promoted and tenured. He is well aware of the statehouse, but with no window, he must picture it in his mind.

I called Neil Foley and arranged to meet him in his garret. I expected to be greeted by an Irish American of thirty-five or forty. Instead, I met a leather-skinned man in his mid-forties sporting a neat ponytail and wearing a bolo tie. His teeth gleamed.

Professor Neil Foley teaches about Texas, and he has written a book about what he calls the "whole black-white, Native American–white, Hispanic-white dyads, and where they shift abruptly in mid-Texas." Texas marks a racial border in the United States. If you slice Texas in half, the eastern part cleaves to the South and historically has been characterized by the same black-white divide that characterizes the South and the North. But in west Texas, the split is between white and Hispanic and between white and Native American. And all of these lines converge in Austin, smack in the middle of the Lone Star State.

They also converge in Neil Foley. In World War II, Foley's mother went to Washington, D.C. A Mexican immigrant, she was bilingual and found work as a secretary in wartime Washington. Foley's dad, a fine young Boston Irishman, had developed a love of the Spanish language, and when he was stationed in D.C., he met Foley's mom. They married, moved to suburban Virginia, and had lots of kids.

"I went to a Jesuit prep school," Foley told me. "And I had my intellectual awakening when I was thirteen and first had contact with the Jesuits. They're the ones who introduced me to classical Greek and Latin, to physics, to public speaking, to all those things that never come up in most public schools. No religious training from them, only constant questioning and interrogation. I was attracted to that. I was attracted to the life of the mind."

As an undergraduate at the University of Virginia, Neil majored in English and watched as the hair grew and students protested in the late 1960s. After college, he went to Georgetown University and got a master's degree in Renaissance studies. From there, Foley began to work on Capitol Hill, and he stayed in government for four years, the last few as an aide to a Republican Senator from Maryland. Maryland in the early 1970s was and still is a very liberal state, and Senator Charles Mathias was one of that now extinct breed of Rockefeller Republicans who were somewhat to the left of today's Clintonite New Democrats.

"One day when I was twenty-four," Foley remembers, "the secretary of the navy came in to talk about some appropriations, and he told me about a program for young fellows like myself to teach on aircraft carriers in the Mediterranean. I thought this sounded pretty cool, so I left four weeks later. I thought I'd be gone a few months, and I ended up teaching on aircraft carriers for the next two years.

"It was a good opportunity to travel. I met my wife in Spain; she was from Michigan of German parentage. I made my living going onto these NATO and SEATO bases teaching English right after the Vietnam War to the all-volunteer forces of mostly blacks, Chicanos, and Puerto Ricans, plus some white kids in the military because they were told it was either the military or jail for drug possession. Teaching *The Great Gatsby* to these kids meant nothing, nothing to a New Yorker from Harlem, or to a Puerto Rican who said, 'Look this isn't my New York, this isn't my understanding of anything American, and frankly I don't give a shit if Jay gets his woman or not.' They asked me, 'Hey, you're Latino, what do you know about your own history? You can tell me all about

Shakespeare or Chaucer, what do you know about your own history, or about the Irish?'

"And I thought, yeah, what do I know? So finally I started reading African American and Latino literature, and after ten years of teaching in Europe and Asia, having gotten married, I decided that I needed a Ph.D. in American studies. From there, I got into the whole black-white, Native American–white dyads, and where they shift abruptly in mid-Texas.

"When I went on the job market in 1990, I wrote eighteen letters, I made the short list at eleven universities and I got eight job offers. Some saw me as doing African American, others saw me as doing ethnic studies, others as race relations or western history. They saw me as someone who could fill lots of different slots. But given my research, Texas just had to have me, and it seemed like the natural place."

In a job market where hundreds of people apply for every opening, the response to Neil Foley was extraordinary. Several things worked in his favor. To begin with, he had an unusual career before turning to academia. He is also charismatic and brilliant. But other factors had less to do with his ability. While affirmative action is under assault throughout the United States, academic departments, particularly in the humanities, are committed to affirmative action. At the same time, humanities departments are interested in work that focuses on minorities, on race/gender/class, and on history from the bottom up.

Not surprisingly, minority academics tend to focus on race/gender/class. As Joyce Appleby noted, people want to learn about themselves. Indeed, the narcissism of academics is no less pronounced than that in any other profession, and academics often start with the question "Who am I?" If the particular "I" is a black woman, it is frequently true that the subject of study will be black women. The same applies for Hispanic men, Irishmen, and white men.

Neil Foley fit a mold of minority candidate studying history and culture of minorities from the bottom up. As such, he was in high demand. At many state schools, special funds are set aside to attract and pay for minority hires. The state of California can hire faculty on a regular departmental budget or it can hire a minority with funds reserved for recruitment of minority faculty. These programs are the professorial side of affirmative action, and unlike undergraduate or law school enrollments, these programs have yet to be challenged in the courts or condemned in the press. Foley received an offer from Berkeley, which asked if he would mind terribly if he were paid with affirmative action funds rather than with departmental money. That way the department could hire two assistant professors instead of the one they had budgeted for.

But as Neil Foley admits, he isn't a typical minority hire, and his ethnicity is very much "constructed" by him. If he wanted to, he could think of himself as Irish or white. He can also think of himself as Chicano or Hispanic. He speaks with some bemusement about the various boxes and categories that he fits, but having lived in Austin for many years, he has come to identify himself more as a Chicano than anything else. And he sees his intellectual work as one aspect of his commitment to social activism.

As he sits in the attic of Garrison Hall, however, Foley wonders about how his role as a professor intersects with his desired role as an activist intellectual. "Not to be cynical, but I think that the university at large does a wonderful job of taking potentially problematic intellectuals out of society and segregating them, isolating them, through the tenure process so that they cease to be a threat to the social order because they become careerist instead of activist.

"A friend of mine, who was also a sixties activist, well, we both think of ourselves as activists in the Chicano movement, the post–civil rights movement that is very much community oriented—not marching in the streets fist-raised, but getting cities not to put toxic waste sites in Chicano communities. My friend said to me, 'We have a graduate student who's been here ten years who's been close to the Zapatista movement,' and my colleague said to me, 'I wish he'd just go ahead and get his Ph.D.; he's been here ten years and he hasn't even gotten to his orals yet, and he'd be much more effective as a professor with a Ph.D.'

"I said to him, I don't agree with you. I feel just the opposite. If he gets his Ph.D., he'll be just like me and you, institutional bureaucrats. We compare our lectures; we sit in our little offices. I don't even have a window looking out on the real world. I sit all day in front of my computer screen. I write a manuscript that's going to be read by other specialists. I'm getting tenure, I get lots of attaboys, but my activism has just been put on hold for six years. Do I even remember what it is anymore?"

When he went to graduate school, Foley thought that the university would give him new opportunities to work for the common good. By the time he went to the University of Michigan to get his Ph.D., he was thirty-five. He didn't want to march in the streets; he wanted to write. But now he finds himself writing not for a wide audience about issues of race in America but for several hundred scholars of Chicano history, or the history of the Southwest, or borderlands history as it is sometimes called. The university doesn't really care what he does outside, whether he helps organize Chicano workers in suburban Austin or whether he speaks Spanish and German to his children. It cares, he says, that he maintain a high-profile scholarly reputation. It cares that he teach his classes, particularly the large survey course on Texas history. And ultimately, he accepts that system because there are few alternatives. He, like anyone else in his mid-forties with a family, needs a place to call home and a steady income. And a university appointment with tenure provides more than a guaranteed salary. It provides security and community.

"You put in your six years of guild dues to get tenure, plus the six years before that to get a Ph.D. You get treated like shit as an assistant professor. You can't do what you want to; you can't write what and how you want; you don't own your life—all in order to get your guild card. And then you have it, and you can do what you want."

To a certain degree, Neil Foley is an exemplar of everything that the conservative critics of the academy detest. Rather than examining a heroic past, he delves into the history of racism in the United States. Rather than fostering a notion of common roots, he examines the differences that separate us. Rather than looking at the high politics of American history, he looks at the men and women whose names and experiences have been forgotten. He casts a cold eye toward the myth of the Alamo, toward the notion that America is a melting pot of inclusiveness, and instead focuses on the oppression of minorities and the hunger for power and money that animated the founders of Texas and the great ranchers.

And he's not shy about expressing his perspective in class. "I teach colonial Texas history here, all three terms. My students want to learn about the Alamo, and they think that the history of Texas begins with Stephen Austin settling east Texas. They want me to teach the creation myths of Texan history, which depend to some extent on the demonization of Mexicans. I tell my students to go see the John Sayles film *Lone Star*. The Alamo myth doesn't work.

"I used to think that my students would hate what I'm teaching. But it turns out that they're big boys and girls. They know the Texas myth is a lot of kaka. They're more sophisticated than their parents. I had a parent call me up, a big-shot lawyer from Dallas. He tells me, 'Professor Foley, my daughter's telling us over dinner that Davy Crockett surrendered at the Alamo.' Now, given that my name's Foley, he probably thought he was talking to a good old boy. He tells me that he's angry but before he calls the history department he wanted to talk to me. After talking to me for a half hour, he probably thought the whole world had gone to hell, and that here in Austin we're all bad apples. Still, my students laugh with me. We have a good time. Four or five are just appalled, but most of them are ready to hear it. They can understand that there are some heroes who forged this republic who guaranteed slavery."

Comments like this are grist for the conservatives' mill.[1] For them, Foley is another radical intent on subverting our culture. But if any of them were to go to Foley's classes, they would find not counterculture hellfire and brimstone but a fairly neutral and comprehensive look at Texas history. That neutrality is itself objectionable to some on the right. For these, the goal of learning history is the inculcation of patriotism, and the goal of the teacher should be to foster a sense of "us" rather than a notion of differences amongst us.

Now Neil Foley himself might be inclined to be more subversive, or activist, in class. But he really can't be. The survey courses are the bread and butter of the history department. The department's budget is pegged to student enrollments, and the state-mandated U.S. or Texas history requirement in effect subsidizes the work of professors throughout the department. But students don't have to fulfill that requirement at the university, and a number of them prefer to satisfy it at a local community college, where the curriculum is taken directly from a textbook and the exam is multiple choice.

Obviously, it is in the interests of the UT-Austin's history faculty that UT-Austin students fulfill the history requirement at UT-Austin. But that means tailoring the survey to the students, at least to some degree. Of course, no one tells Neil Foley how to teach his survey. That would be bad form in an academic department. Notions of intellectual freedom demand that each academic come to his or her own determination of how to teach and what interpretation to give. But no assistant professor who had any hopes of achieving tenure would flagrantly flout the mores of either the department or the students.

As we have seen, the students in Texas, even at the fairly liberal UT-Austin, have certain visions of the past, and they are willing to have these challenged within definite limits. They are willing to be entertained by a long-haired, ethnically diverse professor who tweaks their prejudices and exposes them to a different perspective on the Alamo, but as Kathi Kern found with her students in Kentucky, there is a line. And if professors cross it, students will simply rebel. Whatever Neil Foley's personal agenda, it is constantly mitigated by the demands of his students, his department, and the institution that pays his salary.

The university is a deeply conservative place. It is not ideologically conservative; it is institutionally conservative. It asks both students and faculty to conform to behavior that has been sanctified over time. Students are expected to listen to lectures, speak in seminars, provide written work on demand, and sit for exams. Professors are expected to show up at class, convey knowledge to their students, facilitate their learning, test them, and then grade their achievement. They are also expected to produce knowledge in a manner and form determined by the guild, and the success or failure of their careers depends on their capacity to perform these functions in a manner suitable to their peers.

For individual assistant professors, and to some degree for all professors, insecurity and institutional pressure to do what is expected are far stronger drives than ideological agendas. Careerism, not radicalism, comes first for any assistant professor and for any faculty member who wishes to advance up the ladder. Even tenured professors are not immune from these pressures. Tenure may be a de facto guarantee of employment, but salary is based on performance, and any professor who wants yearly performance raises from the dean or the head of the department has to produce adequate scholarly work. Sitting on university and departmental committees is also expected.

The combined result is exactly what Neil Foley describes. Professors who might see themselves as radical activists find themselves humbled by the institution. As much as they may rail against the inequities of capitalism or the racism that pervades American society, these sentiments are largely confined to their private lives by the demands of their careers.

The same is true for conservative academics who might believe in God and country, who might wish their students to respect the Bible, or who might want to celebrate the noble America that they see under assault. They will find that agenda stymied, not by tenured radicals but by the same forces that constrain Neil Foley.

Ling-Chi Wang is an affable man in his mid-fifties. He teaches ethnic studies at the University of California at Berkeley, and in the 1970s he helped create what was then a new and experimental ethnic studies curriculum. Like Neil Foley, Professor Wang's path to the university was circuitous, and like Neil Foley, he is not entirely what he seems.

"I was born in Fujian, China," he begins, "and I spent my early childhood under the Japanese occupation. Just before Mao took over, as Mao was crossing the Yangtze River, my father decided to move the family to Hong Kong. In Hong

Kong, I received a good British colonial education with a focus on Commonwealth history, Canada, Australia, England. After secondary school, I came to study in the United States, to a very small college in Michigan called Hope College, a Dutch reformed school.

"I received a solid liberal arts education." He smiles wryly at this, and looks at me as if to say, "You see, even though I teach ethnic studies, I don't have the education I bet you thought I did." He continues, "I majored in music composition and minored in philosophy, focusing entirely on western European thought. I took German and Greek in college, and then I started taking ancient languages. My focus was old Babylon, the Old Testament period; I learned Hittite." He pauses and makes a quick digression. "Yet, all this training in European languages and culture didn't change my dissatisfaction with the traditional curriculum at a place like Columbia. It needs to be more inclusive. I'm in favor of a world canon."

He then returns to his story. "I was a graduate student at the University of Chicago, doing Semitic languages, in the 1960s when the surrounding area was the center of lots of protest activity. We felt under siege. There I was studying ancient languages and literature, cloistered in this quadrangle. But I began to take an interest in what was going on outside those walls. Professor Hans Morgenthau started to speak out against the war, and then there was the civil rights movement, so I transferred to Berkeley in 1966, and it was the first time I lived in an area populated by large numbers of Asian Americans.

"I began to wonder if the same issues that were raised by Dr. King in conjunction with blacks might also apply to Asian

Americans. So I'm studying these ancient archeological finds and becoming more aware of the gap between what I was studying and what was going on in the world around me. The rise of ethnic studies gave me an alternative to a career in ancient languages. I took a leave for two years and worked as a community volunteer. In those days, we believed that the real action wasn't in the university but in the community. You had to do something to make a difference. In 1972, I came back to teach one course in Asian American studies, and then I got asked to be full-time. It was a more fluid era." He stops and takes off his glasses, wistfully, and sighs.

"Today, ethnic studies are more deeply involved in theory." The glasses are back on. He tells me of the institutional conservatism of Berkeley. "We put forward candidates for tenure, but the university committee applies its own standards of what is or isn't good scholarship." Activism outside of the department doesn't count or is even seen as a liability. Tenure committees have a narrow definition of what should be rewarded, and as a result, he says, ethnic studies has retreated from engagement in society.

"The academy doesn't look favorably on that kind of engagement. As a scholar, you're supposed to be unattached, neutral, value-free. Now, everything is going back to a presixties era. On the one hand, academics have retreated into intellectualism, knowledge for knowledge's sake, but in reality it's really a surrendering to the pressure of society to become more vocationally, technically oriented. The professional schools get bigger. Universities are becoming vocational schools, and in the process we surrender our academic freedom. Universities always side with the establishment. They are extremely conservative and resist change. I keep asking my colleagues who have retreated to more convoluted highbrow intellectualism what makes their research different from abstract social sciences, and no one's been able to answer that satisfactorily. When I study the role of racism in American society, I cannot ignore the racism around me in society. But I can't say the same for my colleagues."

Both Neil Foley and Ling-Chi Wang see themselves as activists whose activism is effectively neutralized by their guild and their university. In today's political parlance, they are to the left, even the far left. For those who share their politics, the muzzle of academic professionalism is a tragedy; for those who oppose their politics, that muzzle is a godsend, for it is the only thing keeping these tenured radicals from proselytizing to their students.

But if we put aside the question of whether the particulars of their ideologies are good or bad, a more disturbing issue arises. The university in modern America is based on the notion that the free interchange of ideas is vital to the health of democracy. For this reason, the principle of academic freedom is one of the most sacred cows in the academy. In short, professors believe that they must be able to speak and write without fear of dismissal and without the threat of reprisals. If this freedom is not guaranteed, then there is also no guarantee that the university will preserve freedom in general. If students are not allowed to give voice to their opinions, and if professors are not allowed to teach whatever subjects in whatever manner they choose, then we as a society will be one step closer to totalitarianism and thought control.

The limits on academic freedom are debated within the academy, especially in relation to the issue of advocacy. A professor stands in front of a class and announces that she is opposed to the latest American military intervention. Another professor discusses the Fourteenth Amendment and argues that it offers equal protection to homosexuals. Yet another denounces what he takes to be the racism of Joseph Conrad in *Heart of Darkness*.

Clearly, professors take positions such as these all the time. But while individual professors often support the notion that professors should advocate "a personal or political opinion as a way of engaging students,"[2] academic guilds frown at advocacy. The question of advocacy touches nerves in academia because the basis of contemporary academic authority is rooted in the notion that professors are neutral. In its seminal 1915 statement, the American Association of University Professors drew a line between authentic scholarship and political propaganda, a line that could only be maintained by "the disinterestedness and impartiality of [scholarly] inquiry" and by a faculty whose minds are "untrammeled by party loyalties, unexcited by party enthusiasms, and unbiased by personal political ambitions." Only if scholars were perceived as selfless seekers of unbiased truth could academics claim the trust of society. Only if professors refused to be advocates of anything other than the pursuit of objective knowledge would society grant them authority. And finally, only tenure could protect professors from the social pressures that might attempt to coerce them into advocacy.[3]

The sacred cow of academic freedom is, therefore, coupled with another sacred cow, that of neutrality and objectivity. As long as professors accepted the notion that there was absolute truth, then they had to have the freedom to speak it. With the emergence of totalitarianism in the early part of the twentieth century and its flourishing in Soviet Russia, it was not unreasonable for professors to think that they needed protection from those in the larger society who wanted to control what they said, wrote, and even thought.

But in the 1960s, different notions of truth and academia took root. As part of the general skepticism about authority that pervaded Western society in these years, academics began to doubt the existence of absolute truth. They began to suspect that truth was, as the philosopher Michel Foucault was fond of saying, simply a tool of the powerful to control the powerless. "Truth" for Foucault is whatever those with money and influence say it is, and it is always something that benefits those that have at the expense of those that don't.

Professors, swept up in the wholesale questioning of established norms, sought for alternate models. Some intellectuals in nineteenth-century Europe had challenged the ruling classes of the Austro-Hungarian and French empires, and from time to time there had been dissenters within American and English academia. Rather than acting as protectors and preservers of knowledge, many professors in the 1960s and 1970s began to see themselves as intellectuals whose primary responsibility was, in the words of Noam Chomsky, "to speak truth and oppose lies." Truth, for Chomsky, was the opposite of what those with power were saying.[4]

The oppositional relationship between professors and the "establishment" was born from this spirit, and in that respect, many of today's professors who were the product of the 1960s are, in fact, tenured radicals. Academic culture has rewarded those who view power, authority, government, and business with skepticism, and in the humanities, that has meant a proliferation of studies of people who have been kept down by these institutions—namely, women, ethnic or racial minorities, and the poor.

But it isn't as if these tenured radicals are sitting in their offices and busily going about the work of transforming society. They aren't posing much of a threat to the traditional establishment, and they aren't turning undergraduates into fiery protesters, contrary to the frantic warnings of conservative critics. Given how few of Berkeley's graduates go on to careers as leftist activists and how many of them become lawyers, bankers, doctors, and engineers, one could conclude that radical professors have had remarkably little success in converting students. In fact, as we have seen, far from carrying on seminars of radical indoctrination, professors often feel at the mercy of their students, and these students, with their focus on jobs, are leaving college with little ideological fervor of any stripe. Today's students represent a generation of pragmatists who want knowledge that they can apply to their lives. They are looking for skills and certification, and they view their professors' opinions as interesting at best and annoying at worst.

It may have been that for a decade, in the 1970s, professorial activism was rewarded, that the community service of people like Neil Foley or Ling-Chi Wang was discussed by tenure review committees and colleagues and factored favorably into promotions and salary increases.

But if so, it was because for a brief period, academic guilds shifted slightly and placed an abnormally high value on involvement in the larger society. Even during these supposedly radical years, advancement within the academy depended on acceptance by the guild. Professors, therefore, were not rewarded for their activism per se, for their radicalism, or for their engagement with society and their students. They were rewarded for cleaving to the norms and expectations of their guilds.

Today, guild norms have returned to their default setting. While absolute truth has yet to make much of a comeback either within the university or within society at large, sections of the religious right notwithstanding, academic professionalism eschews social activism of all stripes. It looks with equal skepticism on a Chicano professor organizing labor protests in the community and on a conservative Harvard professor like Harvey Mansfield arguing against societal acceptance of homosexuality.

Frustrated activists can be found everywhere. William McAdoo is the chairman of the African American Studies Department at SUNY-Stony Brook. Stony Brook is an example of the shining new campuses that were built in the 1960s. Sitting on dozens of acres ninety miles from New York City in Long Island, the campus is characterized by cinder block and

prefab concrete buildings that were the rage of 1960s archi-
tectural brutalism. Like similar structures at the University of
Massachusetts at Boston and Amherst, or at the University of
California at Santa Barbara, or at hundreds of other schools
across the country, the architecture is fairly depressing.

Before he decamped to academia, McAdoo spent years as
an editor in commercial publishing houses like Viking and
Harper & Row. The day we met he was on and off the phone
coordinating travel plans for speakers who were coming to
campus in honor of black history month. When I asked about
how professors are promoted, he shook his head and spoke
with resignation tinged with anger.

"I have had experiences of sitting at job talks of candidates who are excellent scholars but who are not hired. In
some cases they were not hired because they didn't work
with the paradigms that were dominant, with the methodologies that were dominant. It had nothing to do with the
value of their scholarship. It always pays to find out what
the dominant tendencies are, because you're certainly not
going to get promoted advocating a different perspective. If
you want to do that, you have to go to another department
advocating a different point of view. Academia is a lousy
place to learn how to think; it's a lousy place to learn independence."

SUNY-Stony Brook is the flagship research university of
the New York State higher education system. Professors are
encouraged to produce academic writing, and their teaching
loads reflect that priority. Having fewer courses to teach,
these professors have more time to produce work that will

get them promoted. If they are lucky, they will see no conflict between the general demands of their guilds, the immediate demands of their department, and their own desires as academics. That does not mean, as William McAdoo pointed out, that they will produce innovative, interesting, or provocative work. If anything, it means they will produce work that they believe will earn them the accolades of their peers and so ensure their future security within the university.

Professor McAdoo suffers from the knowledge that his radicalism is institutionally out of place, no matter how heartfelt. Three thousand miles away, in Berkeley, California, radicalism is as common as Baptism in Dallas. But even at UC-Berkeley, the guild limits the questions asked and circumscribes the work done.

The chair of the African American studies department at Berkeley is Percy Hintzen. He is a superb teacher, and it was his class on Malcolm X that struck me as the most open discussion of race in America that I had heard in many years. On a warm day in Berkeley, Hintzen sits in his office with an open shirt. He speaks in a rich baritone, and he looks eerily like Harry Belafonte. "I began high school in the late 1950s in Guyana," he tells me, "and was influenced by Nehru and the leaders of decolonization. Soon after, African Americans and white lower classes in the United States began to challenge Western understanding and fundamental assumptions about worth and reward and belonging, given the objective reality that these did not seem to be working for persons other than the white middle and upper class."

After a long digression into the various causes of inequality in America, Hintzen explains why Berkeley has a multicultural course requirement: "The reality of the U.S. was never one of commonality; it just never was an issue, because everyone was benefiting from the dominant system, except for those defined out of citizenship. But today, now, the U.S. is being forced to recognize that there is not one universal, one uniform America. What we are doing with American Cultures is actually responding to that. Our requirement was started because students began to demand something that spoke to their sense of not knowing what an American is, but knowing that what people say is American is not necessarily them. They say, I want to get me into the definition of America. Students started saying, 'Well I'm not seeing me here at all.' This is particularly true of ethnic and racial minorities, especially in California. What we have done is respond to that by saying that if you speak of America in terms of some sort of uniform America, then you are speaking to nobody. So we have to deal with the reality that America is a very complex place and that other people see America very differently than you. You have to come to some sort of accommodation with different senses of what it means to be an American. But you have to acknowledge the history of difference, and to say that that difference does not mean non-American."

Yet when asked about the bridge between these high ideals and the profession of academia, Hintzen shook his head in disgust. "This is the problem. Academia has become so esoteric that there's a disjuncture between the academic and reality. Academics are now talking to themselves. They're inventing new specialized languages that are so totally irrelevant to the reality of the world. In the social sciences and the humanities, we are talking to ourselves. I believe that there is a certain irrelevance in academia and consequently academia is becoming much more technical rather than intellectual. I believe we must speak to the real problems of the world, but I don't think academics have ever done that.

"It's up to academia to become relevant in terms of dealing with the real issues. I don't think the average ordinary citizen is concerned about postmodernism, but I do think the average ordinary citizen is concerned about why I don't feel as if I'm relevant, why I'm not doing as well as I should, why I don't have choice. And I think that these abstractions ultimately lead back to these concerns. Public scholars are so important because they emerge out of this abstract thinking and translate it to popular culture.

"But if you were an assistant professor writing this way, then you wouldn't get tenure. I'm not sure how one changes the institutional vision to reflect the need for relevance. How does one change the institutional agenda? I think that we have to come to the conclusion that we have to deal with the real world and that the real world can't be dealt with in abstract systems that happen to be a reflection of the mind of the academic rather than the realities of the world."

He paused for a moment and smiled wanly. "We academics are stuck in the nineteenth century."

If even those who fancy themselves radical activists are stymied by the conventions of the guild, then clearly the norms of professionalism are far more entrenched in academia than any particular ideology. As the previous chapter showed, in 1960 no historian or English professor was studying race/class/gender, and there were no courses on African American studies or on multicultural America. For some conservatives, that is to be celebrated and the current trends should be deplored. Not to worry; thirty years from now, the humanities will be dominated by today's graduate students, and as Ling-Chi Wang, Percy Hintzen, and William McAdoo would attest, that work is heading into ever more arcane, theoretical, and quantitative directions. If current signs prove true, the problem in the future won't be the focus on race/class/gender. It will be the inability of any but a few hundred similarly trained scholars to understand what each of them is saying.

The restrictions of guild professionalism do not simply stultify professorial activism. If that were the only consequence, then it might be a spiritual problem for professors but not necessarily a first-order concern for the larger society. But because the rules of the guild have the effect of turning professors away from engagement with social issues on the one hand, and away from teaching on the other, the larger society is harmed, for reasons suggested above and others that will become even more evident in subsequent chapters.

The capstone of the system that keeps professors in this professional box is tenure. Established at the turn of the century to protect academic freedom, tenure has become an entrenched part of the university. Rather than protecting intellectual freedom, however, tenure often impedes it in many ways, and rather than creating a secure environment in which professors can teach and write, tenure has distorted the culture and economy of higher education in destructive ways. Tenure helps keep academics stuck in the nineteenth century. As we have seen, America in the new millennium faces a democratized system of higher education that was inconceivable in the nineteenth century.

Contemporary higher education is placing the system of tenure under great strain. Given the adamant defense of tenure by professors, however, you would think that the system is fine were it not for philistine state legislatures and university trustees who wish to cut budgets and curtail free thought. Events in Texas and Minnesota in 1996 indicate that the system isn't fine, not at all.

5

TENURE

Tenure is easily the most troubling and sensitive issue in academia today. Serious people have disagreed strongly over its merits, and any alternative seems fraught with at least as many perils as the current state of affairs. But though a smaller percentage of faculty members are tenured than at any point in the past decades, professors continue to resist serious discussion of alternatives, and guild organizations angrily denounce schools that experiment with new models of academic employment.

The staunch refusal to embrace innovations and weigh the costs and benefits of tenure makes reform difficult, if not impossible. But as recent controversies in Texas and Minnesota show, tenure cannot continue in its present form, either as an economic system or as an intellectual one. That does not mean that tenure should be abolished everywhere, or that variants of tenure shouldn't be instituted, but the mold of the tenured research scholar simply doesn't fit in many places. In a universe of more than 3,500 institutions, *no* one model will fit. Professors, however, remain wedded to a narrow image of what they do and an even narrower image of how they should be employed. That narrow, parochial allegiance to one form of employment and one definition of academic work was nowhere more in evidence than during the disputes in Texas and Minnesota in 1995 and 1996.

In theory, the tenure system creates a barrier against dismissal; it buttresses academic freedom; and it also places professorial self-governance at the heart of the university. After the establishment of tenure earlier in the century, professors, not administrators, legislators, or students, became the arbiters of their own employment and promotion.

Across the country, tenure faces challenges. Some of these challenges are hostile to academic freedom and intellectual life, but many are not. Yet professors rarely distinguish between legitimate questions about tenure and unreasonable attacks. That knee-jerk defense squelches serious discussion. As an issue that sets the contemporary economics of higher education against one of the most hollowed tenets of academeme, tenure demands an intensive examination on the part of professors, administrators, and the state legislators who allocate the funds that pay the salaries. Academic freedom and job security are vital goods, for any professor and for society. But they are not absolute goods, and to the degree that the system of tenure negates other goods, it needs to be reconsidered. And while aiding those that have it, tenure does not necessarily protect either academic freedom or job security for the vast ranks of the untenured.

Every year, sixty-seven thousand students enroll at the University of Minnesota. The main campus of the university at

Minneapolis–St. Paul is often called the state's "crown jewel," and Minnesotans refer to it simply as the "U." Most of its students attend the main campus, while the rest can be found at satellite campuses in Duluth, Morris, and Crookston. In order to educate these sixty-seven thousand men and women, the state of Minnesota employs three thousand professors of various ranks. In 1997–98, the state legislature allocated $572 million for the University of Minnesota, a 23-percent increase from the budget the year before.[1] Yet few people at the University of Minnesota were celebrating, because in 1996 the university was mired in a controversy over tenure that left the faculty shaken, the public wary, and the image of the school tarnished.

In the fall of 1995, the university found itself facing a steep operating loss. Though the state of Minnesota is committed to generous public financing of higher education, its allocations for education have barely kept up with rising costs.[2] Like government, many of these costs are driven upwards by expanding layers of bureaucracy. At a state school such as Minnesota, there are numerous departments, both research and administrative, that touch only indirectly on student life. Tuition dollars provide only a portion of the needed revenue, because at state schools, tuition is kept low in order to honor the commitment to education for all.

In December 1995, the regents of the university proposed that the rules governing faculty tenure be altered to allow the administration more latitude in laying off tenured faculty. The suggestion was made quietly, and the response was muted. In the spring, the Faculty Senate took up these suggestions, and at the end of May 1996 it recommended that the tenure code should remain as is. The lone concession to budgetary issues was a proposal that the base pay of tenured professors could be cut, slightly, under extraordinary circumstances.[3]

The twelve members of the board of regents are appointed by the state legislature. In 1996, the board was chaired by Tom Reagan, who was particularly eager to gain the power to fire tenured professors whose departments had been closed and whose programs had been discontinued. At first glance, that doesn't seem unreasonable. For instance, not all departments continue to attract significant undergraduate enrollments for their courses. In recent years, certain colleges have shut down their geography departments and folded courses in other departments like anthropology and history.

But under the tenure code of almost every school, closing a department does not release the administration from the responsibility to pay faculty tenured in departments that have since been shut down. Tenure is like a major-league baseball contract; the school has to honor its commitment whether or not faculty members are teaching, provided that the reason for their lack of teaching is the school's unwillingness to have them teach an underenrolled course. If they aren't teaching because they refuse to show up to class, the school does have recourse and can even fire a tenured professor for incompetence or "moral turpitude," a phrase that covers anything from chronic absence from class to sexually harassing a student.

The rigid interpretation of tenure was developed in response to university administrators who until World War I would fire professors for saying things that administrators didn't like or for using resources that administrators wished to use differently. Even after tenure had been effectively instituted throughout the country, professors were at times fired for what they wrote and said. Justifying the firing of professors suspected of Marxist views in the late 1940s, the president of Yale, Charles Seymour, acerbically remarked, "There will be no witch hunts at Yale because there will be no witches."[4]

The faculty at the University of Minnesota rejected the regents' proposal because from their perspective, the plan was the latest attempt by university administrators to use the claim of financial exigency to wrest control of education from the professors. Humanities faculty would have been hit hard under the plan, because humanities enrollments have been on a steady decline for decades. At the "U," two departments were abolished in the early 1990s: humanities and linguistics.[5]

At the same time, the budgetary shortfalls had caused real problems. The average class size ballooned in the 1980s, and undergraduates were lucky to attend a course with fewer than a hundred students. Student advising and recruiting also suffered, as student/advisor ratios rocketed upwards. There were widespread stories of students packed anonymously into classes, passively taking notes, and then sitting for multiple-choice exams. With so many students for each professor and insufficient numbers of teaching assistants, it was simply not feasible for a professor to grade anything but a multiple-choice test.[6]

Large class sizes are endemic at state universities. At Berkeley, Ling-Chi Wang laughed at the absurdity of trying to reach the hundreds of students in his lecture courses. He sent his own children to liberal arts colleges in the East and said that they were receiving a better education than his Berkeley students ever could, at least in terms of access to professors and seminars in which they could work through ideas with a small, focused group.

Throughout the summer of 1996, the regents, the Faculty Senate, and the president of the "U," Nils Hasselmo, exchanged letters that mapped out their respective positions. Hasselmo leaned toward the faculty, and he informed the regents that his administration would oppose layoffs of tenured faculty whose programs had been discontinued. But the regents pushed ahead. They believed that tenure rigidly construed was preventing the "U" from allocating resources on the basis of student demand. As Chairman Tom Reagan explained, "Our current code doesn't give the university the flexibility to make the changes demanded by our quest for quality. It doesn't give the university the flexibility to respond to the increasing competition for students, for teachers, and for money."[7]

In early September, the regents unveiled their plan to the faculty. Under the regents' proposed revisions of the tenure code, professors could be fired or have their salaries cut if the administration deemed it necessary to shift resources away from one department or division to another. That meant that if the deans or the regents determined that, say, the school of communications needed more money to cover its increasing student enrollments, then it would be possible not only to cut the budget of the anthropology department but to cut the salaries or even fire tenured anthropology professors whose teaching services were no longer in heavy demand.

What really inflamed the faculty and alarmed the American Association of University Professors was the language of an additional clause. The regents also suggested that it should be easier to discipline professors for not maintaining a "proper attitude of industry and cooperation."[8]

If the regents had stuck to the argument that the tenure code made serious discussion of university budgetary priorities impossible, they might have succeeded in forcing changes, or at least in forcing the faculty to come up with proposals of their own. But the phrase "proper attitude" was incendiary to a faculty with a collective memory of McCarthyite pressures and arrogant administrators who felt free to dictate professional conduct to university professors. "If you have a provision that basically says people can be fired if they don't show the proper attitude," commented one Minnesota professor, "I don't think really you're talking about a university anymore. You might well be talking about a military unit of some kind, but universities are intended to encourage independent thinking, which is sometimes accompanied, unfortunately, by cantankerous behavior."[9]

Both the faculty and Hasselmo reacted. Little more than a week after the regents announced their plan, the faculty began to organize a union drive. The move toward unionization was purely tactical. If enough professors signed cards asking for a union election, Minnesota state labor laws would be triggered, and the state would issue an ordinance freezing all employment conditions at the university until the union could form and bargain collectively. That would prevent, at least temporarily, the regents from acting on their plan. Hasselmo, a former professor himself, sided with the faculty.

By October, the drama unfolding at the "U" was national news. The press was not favorable, and while the faculty came off as truculent, the regents appeared like bullies. Faced with an intense backlash, the regents began to retreat. Major factions in "U" politics, including the alumni association, urged the regents to end the dispute before further public relations damage occurred.

In mid-October, the dean of the law school, Thomas Sullivan, offered a modified tenure plan, billed as a compromise, that would have allowed salary cuts but not layoffs. After voting 121–1 against the regents' plan, the Faculty Senate tentatively endorsed Sullivan's proposal. Soon after, the governor of Minnesota, Arne Carlson, described by many as an ardent supporter of tenure reform, criticized the regents for their insensitivity. He threatened that state appropriations for the "U" could be jeopardized if the fight continued.[10]

Finally, in early November, the regents blinked. Tom Reagan announced that he would ask the regents to approve the Sullivan modified plan, which in effect preserved lifetime employment for tenured professors. Meanwhile, the state ordered that employment conditions be frozen until union representatives were elected. There was widespread talk in Minneapolis–St. Paul of putting a two-year moratorium on further discussions about tenure. "It is the sense of this board, as I see it," said Tom Reagan after announcing the regents' decision, "that we will not be revisiting the tenure code for at least a year and a half and probably never."[11]

Though the professors had won this round, the financial issues are real, and while state allocations in Minnesota are likely to be ample for years to come, how those resources are distributed within the university remains an unsettled and contentious question. In the view of State Representative Becky Kelso, "There is not enough money for the status quo, and there hasn't been for a while and no reason to think that there's going to be. The University of Minnesota is a classic case of a situation where they're doing too much of everything and not enough of anything to maintain quality."[12]

In the eyes of many faculty members, that is heresy. History professor Hy Berman felt the regents and the state legislature were acting in concert to usurp the role of the faculty in setting academic priorities, a job they are not qualified to perform, says Berman. "If you had to have heart transplant surgery, would you go to an MBA to have that done? Would you go to a person with a Ph.D. in education to have that done? No. You go to the best heart surgeon you could find. Similarly, in the academic enterprise, are you going to go to a chair of the board of regents who is a political hack to determine academic content?"[13]

In trying to dilute the entitlement of lifetime employment, the Minnesota regents ran squarely into one of the cherished privileges of the faculty, and the faculty fought tenaciously and for the moment successfully to retain that right. At the same time that the fight was being lost by the regents in Minnesota, however, another contest was being fought and won by state officials in Texas.

Unlike in Minnesota, the state legislature and the regents in Texas questioned the very aspect of tenure that Professor Hy Berman defended: the ability of faculty to set the academic agenda. Instead of basing the challenge primarily on financial grounds, the Texas State Senate suggested that the tenure system does not adequately address the problem of professorial incompetence.

At the top tier of the state university system in Texas—the A&M campuses and the University of Texas campuses—around 60 percent of the faculty are tenured. At all state campuses in Texas combined, that figure drops below 50 percent. Out of nearly nine thousand tenured professors in public colleges in Texas, only eight were fired between 1990 and 1995, three for poor performance. In the past twenty-five years, UT-Austin has fired only one tenured professor for incompetence. Texas is not alone. In the entire United States, only fifty professors are fired annually.[14]

These statistics bothered Senator Bill Ratliff, a Republican from Mount Pleasant, in east Texas, just outside Texarkana. "It's just against human nature that such a high percentage of employees are performing so well," he commented. "I hear of professors so on automatic pilot that they've not changed their syllabus in twelve years."[15] Ratliff was the chairman of the Texas Senate Education Committee in the spring of 1996 when he introduced a recommendation that tenure in the UT system be overhauled.

Ratliff's proposal followed a 1995 decision by the regents of the Texas A&M system to institute new guidelines for tenure that mandate a "post-tenure review" procedure at each campus. In essence, "post-tenure review" means that tenured professors would be subject to regular performance assessments, and that their continued employment would depend on favorable evaluations by students and colleagues. The A&M system in Texas is the more conservative of the two top-tier systems. While the A&M faculty didn't embrace post-tenure review, their outcry against it was muted in comparison to the furor that erupted at UT-Austin when Senator Ratliff made his proposal.[16]

Of course, Ratliff didn't exactly shy away from inflammatory statements, and his attitude toward the faculty at UT-Austin fell somewhere between scorn and condescension. A conservative politician from a conservative area, Ratliff seemed to embody that tried-and-true American value of anti-intellectualism.[17] While he suggested a plan that would demand the dismissal of any professor who received "below standard" marks two years in a row, he also called on the faculty to come up with a suitable plan of their own. Meeting with an antagonistic group of professors drawn from the Faculty Advisory Council, Ratliff tut-tutted them like errant children. "I'll tell you folks, you're your own worst enemy." He warned them to come up with a system that would get rid of incompetent teachers. "It's the perception that [tenure's] a gravy train," he said. "Every one of you knows one or more members of your department that either ought to get kicked in the rear, or they ought to be sent packing. I want the incompetents removed."[18]

Ratliff wasn't the first state representative to launch an assault on the faculty at Austin. The Texas legislature has always been more conservative than the faculty up the hill, and at various times speakers in the statehouse have railed against the professors at UT for undermining American values, for opening the floodgates to communism, for being a group of coddled elitists.

But Ratliff's plan was more than just another fulmination. There were rumblings on campus that posttenure review wasn't really Ratliff's idea at all, and it was a bit odd that this senator from Mount Pleasant, with no prior record indicating that he held strong views on higher education, should chose to make his mark with this issue. Some speculated that the idea of posttenure review came from the chancellor of the UT system, William Cunningham, who may have wanted to have more leeway to corral dissident faculty. One prominent defender of the tenure status quo, Professor Alan Cline of the computer science department, had been one of the most vocal opponents of the proposed naming of a campus building for Jim Bob Moffet, a large donor who was the chairman of mining giant Freeport-McMoRan.[19] Seeing a conspiracy, some faculty believed that Cunningham and Jim Bob urged Ratliff to introduce the proposed reforms.

Whether or not that was the impetus, the faculty were convinced that talk of quality control was simply a clever screen for thought control. "On the surface it looks pretty mild," Cline said. "What I'm interested in is what lies beneath the surface."[20] A philosophy professor elaborated, "Tenure is designed to give people the opportunity to invent new teaching methods, work on research, and break new barriers of knowledge. Changes could seriously hurt and weaken the present system."[21] Others were less diplomatic. "Forty years ago, universities were purged during the McCarthy era," charged one irate faculty member. "The people who were behind that are the same kind of people who are behind this today."[22]

As with Minnesota, plans to change tenure divided the university. The president, Robert Berdahl, and the provost, Mark Yudof, rushed to assure the faculty that at worst, a watered-down version of Ratliff's plan would be instituted. Provost Yudof said that he "would be surprised if more than 5 percent of the tenured faculty" would have any difficulty getting adequate marks, no matter what type of posttenure review were instituted.[23]

In the meantime, Senator Ratliff moved on to the finance committee and was replaced at the education committee by Senator Teel Bivins, a Republican from Amarillo, in the panhandle of west Texas. While Bivins remained committed to forcing the UT faculty to institute some sort of reform by early 1997, he evinced a greater willingness to let the university design those reforms itself.

In late September, Chancellor Cunningham issued his plan, and with slight modification, it went into effect in early 1997. Under it, tenured faculty will be reviewed every five years rather than annually as Ratliff initially wanted. The review will take both research and teaching into consideration, and it will be conducted by a committee of tenured peers.

While many faculty continued to bristle at this erosion of absolute tenure, others were relatively sanguine about its effects. "Professors are already reviewed annually by deans and department chairs to determine pay raises," said Professor Carolyn Boyd, chair of the history department. "Posttenure review is not that different than what already exists." And though the new process does allow for dismissal, Boyd and others doubted that a committee of tenured peers would ever vote on removing one of their own.[24]

During these months, many voices outside the university criticized tenure for its inefficiency. In the eyes of Senator Ratliff and the supporters of posttenure review, professorial employment practices protect incompetents.[25] The public view of tenure in Texas has always been one of raised eyebrows. Giving people a lifetime guarantee of employment seemed to be a recipe for sloth, and in a state where welfare was coming under fire for undermining the work ethic, tenure wasn't likely to enjoy widespread support. To some degree, these attitudes can be found throughout the United States. For much of the public, tenure just doesn't seem right, particularly in an era of corporate downsizing. The fact that other than judges, most high school teachers, and government bureaucrats few people in America have job security doesn't endear academics to the public at large.

All the more reason, respond tenured faculty, to defend the institution of tenure. Between corporate downsizing and public scorn of much of what professors do, the only thing preserving scholarship and academic freedom is tenure. It would be a great mistake, wrote David Braybrooke, professor of liberal arts at UT, if universities were managed like corporations. "A university should be a milieu for encouraging faculty and students alike to join in the advancement and diffusion of knowledge. Imposing inappropriate demands on such a milieu can easily cast a blight on it and dry up the encouragement."

In addition to the negative impact on undergraduate education, Braybrooke pointed to the imperative for academic freedom. "Tenure safeguards members of the milieu against reprisals from their colleagues. . . . Attacks on academic freedom often begin, not with outsiders, not with university administration, but with factions within departments." Posttenure review, therefore, carried out by a jury of one's peers, would allow for reprisals based on different scholarly methodologies and ideologies.[26]

As it has turned out, at UT-Austin, posttenure review will likely be a recipe for the status quo. While there is the appearance of change, until a committee of tenured professors decides to cashier one of their peers, posttenure review will amount to little more than a rubber stamp. The University of Texas has tried to build a world-class university, and over the past thirty years, it has spent enormous sums of money luring star faculty to Austin and building facilities to house them. If it becomes known that a job offer at Austin may amount to nothing more than a five-year contract, then that money will have been wasted, much to the embarrassment of the university and to the state as well. The faculty were able to raise that specter successfully, and the legislature backed off, having achieved a hollow victory.

These episodes in Texas and Minnesota are two examples of a national trend. Dozens of states have mounted some sort of assault on tenure in the mid-1990s.[27] Unlike the ideological challenges of the past, the questions being raised about tenure by legislators and university administrators are driven more by economic concerns. College costs continue to escalate at the same time the country is embracing the notion that all Americans have a right to some college education. State expenditures on education barely keep pace with inflation, yet public universities and colleges simply cannot raise prices to meet expenses because with each tuition hike, higher education becomes unaffordable to thousands of would-be students. The result: State schools cannot both pay tenured faculty and keep tuition sufficiently low to satisfy the demand for access to all.[28]

Many tenure absolutists respond that claims of financial difficulty are essentially a clever ruse. Opponents of tenure, defenders say, are the same anti-intellectuals as those in the 1920s and the 1950s, but now they have found a way to cloak their agenda behind a facade of financial exigency and the public good. That argument has some merit. It would be easy to impugn the motives of many of the legislators backing proposals to alter or abolish tenure, and many of them have little love for what they take to be the left-wing bias of academics.

In addition, the attempts of administrators and legislators to make the university more businesslike, as one official at the University of Oregon declared, are not easily reconcilable with the demands of scholarship. The president of the University of Illinois says that he wants the system to be "run more like a business," and that means whatever isn't marketable isn't supportable.[29] Not all topics are in demand. Subjects like Ming pottery, Khmer architecture, Mayan math, and the branding practices of the Pilgrims don't lend themselves to large lecture courses. And in the post–cold war world, the more arcane aspects of the hard sciences are financially pressed as well. Only tenure and academic freedom allow professors to preserve knowledge about topics that are not in wide demand.

But defenders of tenure go even farther. Rather than concede that the explosion of student enrollments and the rapid expansion of higher education might have disrupted the economy of higher education, professors brush aside questions of economy and retreat to principle. In an open letter to the Texas House of Representatives, the American Association of University Professors wrote the following:

> Academic tenure is not well understood. It is often mistaken for a lifetime job guarantee, with easy hours and no particular requirements of achievement. Since none of the rest of us get that kind of guarantee in life, it is natural to wonder why professors should have it so easy. But that's not what tenure means. Academic tenure protects professors from being fired *unreasonably*, for teaching or inquiring into an area that might be politically or commercially unpopular. As the University of Texas System Regents' statement acknowledges: "Throughout history, the process of exploring and expanding the frontiers of learning has necessarily challenged the established order. That is why tenure is so valuable, not merely for the protection of individual

faculty members, but also as an assurance to society that the pursuit of truth and knowledge commands our first priority." . . . As a legislator, you have no doubt recognized that it is sometimes inconvenient to guard some of our most precious individual rights—like the right to freedom of expression, and the freedom to learn. Likewise, academic freedom might be inconvenient—it might make it harder for a university to plan outcomes and products the way a corporation would. But a university is not a corporation; it should be an oasis from the marketplace where new ideas—new curiosities—get a chance to be aired, and if worthy to grow. Academic tenure protects such inquiries. We urge you . . . to protect academic tenure.[30]

To say "defenders of tenure" is itself somewhat misleading. It would be like saying "defenders of democracy in the United States." It is extremely rare to meet a professor who doesn't defend tenure. It is equally rare to meet a graduate student who doesn't aspire to tenure, and it is unusual to encounter an underemployed adjunct who isn't hoping for a tenured position. Tenure in academia is an article of the scholarly faith.

Those within academia who question tenure are treated with the withering scorn reserved for apostates. Richard Chait, a professor of education at Harvard, has written widely about alternatives to tenure, and he headed a Pew Foundation project that examined different models for a tenureless university. Chait is not only criticized; he is excoriated. One opponent charged that Chait was "selling snake oil."[31] In conversations with academic deans and department chairs, I have been greeted with raised eyebrows, incredulous stares, and then frosty condescension when I asked if alternatives to tenure had any merit. Discussions about changing tenure are as unwelcome in academia as discussions of women priests are in the Catholic Church.[32]

It is possible to question tenure without being an opponent of academic freedom. Early in the century, the courts had not yet extended speech protection to citizens of states. For instance, until the late 1960s, a professor at a public college who shouted "Death to America. Long live Mao. Lenin is wonderful" in a university rest room could have been fired by school administrators. As a result of a series of Supreme Court decisions, the speech of that professor is now protected, regardless of tenure. Those protections apply only to teachers at public colleges. A private school, like Harvard or Brigham Young University, can still insist on codes of conduct and terminate the contracts of faculty members who violate them. But given that the preponderance of students now attend public colleges, legal precedents in the public realm determine much of what is acceptable at private schools.

Academic freedom is clearly important. The AAUP rightly points to the necessity of preserving knowledge and truth if our society is to remain open and relatively free. In addition, some types of scholarship simply can't survive if free-market rules are applied. The preservation of knowledge is a public good, like interstate roads and the Federal Aviation Administration. But if the courts now guarantee a degree of free expression that was not legally protected when tenure was established, then tenure may not be as essential to academic freedom as it once was.

In fact, tenure may now inhibit as much freedom as it protects. That in itself is reason enough to reform the system. Equally troubling is what the bulk of tenured professors do with their freedom.

Most professors reading these lines would respond with incredulity.[33] Tenure, the capstone of academic freedom, stifling free expression? Well, yes. As David Braybrooke pointed out, academic colleagues are not necessarily the fairest of judges. In his admittedly exaggerated but nonetheless evocative novels on academic life, David Lodge has shown just how petty and vindictive professors can be, how territorial they are, and to what lengths they will go to destroy the careers of rivals. In theory, tenure protects professors from the more extreme consequences of academic vindictiveness. For those professors who have tenure, that is certainly true. The problem is that a smaller percentage of professors now have tenure, and the number is declining yearly. Overall, in the early 1990s, 47 percent of professors were either tenured or "tenure track," while 45 percent were nontenured and not eligible for tenure. At research universities, the numbers favored tenured faculty, with more than 70 percent tenured or in jobs with tenure as a possibility. At two-year colleges, nearly 70 percent were not tenured and not on "tenure track."[34] We have already seen the intense competition for entry-level jobs among graduate students, but fewer of those assistant professors are becoming tenured, and for economic reasons, fewer schools are even hiring new professors on the "tenure track."

Tenure requires a considerable commitment of a school's financial resources. At Ivy League schools such as Yale and Harvard, barely 10 percent of junior faculty are ever granted tenure, even if their jobs are technically "tenure track." Many tenured chairs require a pool of money before a position can be created and filled. These positions, known as "endowed chairs," require as much as $5 million in order to generate enough income annually to cover a salary of $100,000 as well as health and pension benefits, administrative assistance, and a research budget. Most professorships are not endowed chairs, but even at a state college, administrators realize that the decision to grant tenure is a decades-long financial commitment that will remain as a fixed cost regardless of the economic health of the school. That means that many schools shy away from tenure and instead offer nonrenewable yearly contracts to some and adjunct contracts to others. For adjuncts, the school doesn't even need to pay benefits, so the cost is that much lower.

The economy of tenure is obviously more complex than this description suggests, but these economic calculations bear directly on academic freedom. Tenure has always been a prize, but in today's academic job market tenured positions are ever smaller islands in an ever larger sea. Their value has increased significantly because the demand far exceeds the supply. To an alarming degree, that allows for professors with tenure to determine what those without it say and write.

In order to receive tenure, an assistant professor must pass muster first with his or her department. At the end of three years, assistant professors are evaluated, and if they survive that evaluation, then at the end of five, six, or seven years, they are "brought up" for tenure. Almost all universities have three official criteria for promotion and tenure: research, teaching, and service. Research is what a professor writes; teaching is performance in the classroom; and service is anything from committee work to fund-raising. In practice, however, most departments promote on the basis of research, research, and research. As any assistant professor will attest, good teaching and a plethora of service will be of little avail if the research doesn't satisfy certain standards. Bad teaching just might hurt one's chances at certain schools, but while there are many stories of bad teachers getting promoted on the basis of esteemed research, few great teachers get promoted without a paper trail of books and articles.

These writings have to be approved both by the department and by the entire community of scholars in the discipline. When a school is considering a candidate for tenure, it is normal to solicit letters from established scholars throughout the country, many of whom may not know the candidate but will have read his or her writings. When evaluating the candidate's scholarship, the referees will apply their sense of the norms of the field. In fact, this is but one of many periods when a professor will be judged in this way. At each stage of their career, professors are assessed by peers and those above them. In order to get a piece of writing published by an academic journal or a university press, it must pass through two to five anonymous reviewers who will test the writing against the standards of the discipline.

These norms are the rules of the guild. They are in many ways arbitrary, but they are also binding. Any junior professor who flouts the conventions of the community of scholars does so at great professional peril. These conventions are enforced not just when someone comes up for promotion but every time an assistant professor attends a conference with senior colleagues, and each time the junior faculty member has a conversation about scholarship with the elders of the department. As Neil Foley said, until you get tenure, your life isn't your own, and neither is your work.

What ends up happening is a subtle series of decisions that amount to self-censorship. Combined with the not-so-subtle decision to refuse promotion to those who violate guild norms, the overall effect of the tenure system is to protect the academic freedom of the tenured at the expense of the freedom of the untenured.

An untenured faculty member is perfectly free to teach and write what he or she wants, as long as that person is willing to become unemployed as a result. Given the rigid structure and hierarchies of academia, the freedom is purely symbolic. Thus, an untenured professor is no more free to express himself than an employee of a corporation is. A middle manager at General Electric is "free" to tell his superiors they're idiots, but he will likely find himself out of a job. So too will a junior faculty member who explicitly criticizes the work or ideas of the senior faculty who will decide on his promotion.

If the job market were less tight, the pettiness of individual academics would be offset by the demand for qualified scholars. But in an era when each job is precious, most junior faculty will not risk the censure of those above them. The penalty of losing the job, in the form of not having the contract renewed, is simply too great. This affects the form of the research as well as the type of subjects. Like graduate students, junior faculty are sensitive to what is "hot" in their field. They will try to do work that the community of scholars in their discipline will sanction. If that means framing the question in terms of race/gender/class, then that is how it will be framed. Just as middle managers will go golfing with their bosses whether or not they like golf, so too will assistant faculty chose topics to research that are acceptable and that will get them promoted.

Scholarship is narrowly defined. It looks a certain way, and each field develops its own definitions of good scholarship. In history, the emphasis is on extensive archival documentation, on original manuscripts that substantiate the thesis. In English or sociology, the emphasis tends to be on theory and the rigor with which that theory is developed. Scholarship speaks to other scholars, and most scholarly writing assumes a good deal of prior knowledge of jargon and concepts that usually litter academic writing.

The narrow definition of scholarship excludes many types of writing. For instance, in history, an article in the *American Historical Review* or a book published by Harvard University Press is an important credential for tenure. But an article in *Harper's* magazine or a book published by a commercial publisher is not. The first two are peer-reviewed scholarly publishers, the latter are more commercial and are directed at the general reader. At a conference held at the University of Chicago in the spring of 1997, several professors scoffed at the notion of writing for "glossy magazines" or commercial publishers. What can be found there isn't scholarship, they said; it's popularized, oversimplified pap. As one presenter said of academics as opposed to journalists, "We are not in the gist business."

If a young professor were to spend her time writing for a local newspaper about some pressing community issue, or another were to take his time to explain to Washington politicians why the cold war is not a good paradigm for military spending today, they might be doing society either much harm or much good. In neither case would those activities count in their favor in the decision to grant tenure. Scholarship is defined by academics as something different from a rigorous essay in *The New Yorker* or an impassioned op-ed in a local paper. Here again, academic freedom is a much more limited concept than it at first appears to be.

It is true, as Neil Foley said, that once you earn tenure, you have your guild card and can then do what you want. But it is a rare individual who can cleave closely to a restrictive set of norms for fifteen years of graduate school and assistant professorship without internalizing those norms. By the time the tenured professor has passed through all the necessary hoops, he will probably adhere closely to those norms for the rest of his life. While tenured professors do have the genuine freedom to write and say what they wish, few wish to exercise that freedom in ways that depart from the way their colleagues exercise it.

The situation is even worse for adjuncts. Without even the promise of a full-time job with benefits, they are left to cobble together a living that may require teaching at three or four different community colleges, hours of commuting to and fro, and little time left in the day. As we shall see later, the life of an adjunct is at best strained, and one of the hardest aspects is the vicious circle that most adjuncts find themselves in. They must teach to survive, but in teaching so much, they have no time to do the research that is their only hope of ever getting a full-time job. Very few schools will hire a full-time faculty member on the basis of good teaching. There are signs that this is changing, but it remains that in most places, one is hired based on research. Adjuncts, then, have no economic stability, and they have no time to enjoy the luxury of academic freedom. They can say what they want, but they still have to eat.

This leads to the other major problem with tenure today: It gets in the way of good teaching. Many tenured professors laud the holistic connection between good teaching and good research. Research, they say, makes them more connected to their subject. I don't doubt that many tenured professors experience a deep connection between their work and their teaching, but it's worth questioning the formula that good teaching depends on active research. Thousands of high school teachers do no research whatsoever, yet they are frequently better teachers than their college counterparts, even if they are not "scholars." Scholarship may improve teaching, but it is not a necessary component of good teaching.

Because a professor's career rises or falls on the basis of writing, teaching is frequently seen as a distraction. That is in direct contradiction to what many state universities, community colleges, and liberal arts institutions need. In the hundreds of colleges that have sprung up in the past decades, in community colleges and expanded state campuses, the primary need is teaching. Students enrolling at these schools often have poor high school educations and limited reading skills. They need to be taught the basics of writing and the general history that most of us deem essential to functioning as an informed citizen. They need, in short, dedicated teachers who will spend considerable time in class and out on making sure these skills are developed.[35]

One of the results of the academic job crisis, however, is that graduate students and recent Ph.D.'s are taking any job they can get. An opening for an assistant professor of English at the University of Oklahoma at Stillwater attracts nearly as many applicants as a job at Harvard or Yale. Having gotten a job at Stillwater, a graduate student from Yale is likely to think of herself as exiled[36] and is likely to look for a way to return to the elite institutions of scholarship that she feels she has been trained for. The only way to do that is by producing research that is read by established scholars at elite institutions, and the only way to produce this research is to be given lighter teaching loads by the university.

As a result, junior professors put pressure on places like Stillwater to give them more generous leaves, more summer research money, and fewer courses a term to teach. Now, state higher education systems that have recently expanded have done so because there are more students to teach. The need they are supposed to fill is to provide undergraduates with training. But they also wish to attract good faculty, as any institution would like to attract the best possible employees. Schools therefore respond to the requests of their junior faculty and lessen teaching loads.

It used to be typical for professors to teach four or even five courses a term. Now, at elite research universities like Harvard or Berkeley, two courses per term is the standard. That leaves the professor free to pursue research. That does not leave the professor free to pursue any research that he or she finds interesting. Less teaching provides more time, not more intellectual freedom. And it is time that many professors don't even use for research. That leads to what academics call the "deadwood problem"—professors who receive tenure and then proceed to do no research, no writing, and mediocre teaching for decades thereafter.

Minimal teaching loads have been one lightning rod of criticism of professors, especially in the recent assaults in states such as Minnesota and Texas. Professors are said to be bilking both public and private universities by extracting maximum payment for minimum work.[37] If anything, however, most professors, even those who teach only two courses per term, are overworked. The pressure to produce research is constant. Writing an article or a book does not take into account weekends or evenings, and the weight given to research over teaching means that professors try to minimize their classroom and administrative time in order to attend to research.

In the past decade some departments have begun to move away from a research emphasis to a teaching emphasis. Some departments do in fact promote professors on the basis of teaching. In those places, student evaluations are taken very seriously, and members of the tenure committee go and attend lectures and classes taught by the candidate. The teach-

discussed by the committee,

ing style re solicited from students to get

and in candidate's teaching ability. But

an eve ion, and many faculty are uncom-

such ng being weighted so heavily.

forta abolition of tenure altogether. One of

Florida Gulf Coast University, in Fort

the d in the fall of 1997. There are no

M ead, everyone is hired on multiyear con-

two to five years. There is no impediment

al of these contracts, but then there is no im-

tting faculty go when their contracts expire.[38]

nnington College, in Vermont, was facing a dire

situation, with a $1 million deficit and plummeting

nt enrollments. While higher education as a whole has

anded, small, rural liberal arts colleges have faced diffi-

culties attracting students. With high tuition, no significant

sports teams, and isolated settings, liberal arts schools have

seen the pool of applicants shrink. In 1988, Bennington had

600 students, but in 1995, there were only 285. In response,

the president of the college in conjunction with the board of

trustees fired a third of the tenured professors, abolished

most of the departments, and placed all remaining faculty on

multiyear contracts. While the AAUP protested vigorously,

student applications began to climb, costs were cut, and a

new premium was placed on innovative teaching.[39] And at

the University of Phoenix, faculty members rarely have

Ph.D.'s; they don't have tenure; and even in humanities

fields, they are hired almost entirely for
teach and not the research they have done

Scholarship and teaching can thrive wit
the opposition to reform remains as implac
response to the many debates over tenure
Arthur Raines, the president of the Georgeto
the AAUP, wrote the following in an editorial p
Washington Post:

> Many schools are in dire financial straits, and tenu
> an impediment for administrators to hire and fire facu
> based on enrollments, expenses, demand for a particula
> class or whatever. But the tenure system also provides
> important benefits. It allows a faculty member to embark
> on an academic career and invest himself in an institu-
> tion with the expectation of building a research or teach-
> ing program that will bring credit to both the faculty
> member and the institution. . . . It is true that an experi-
> enced 60-year-old full professor with an international
> reputation may cost as much as two inexperienced and
> untried instructors. But whom would you choose to edu-
> cate your kids? . . . The very best of bright new faculty
> will always opt for a tenure-track opening, which offers
> the potential for a stable position, over one that is not el-
> igible for tenure. It's unfortunate for higher education in
> America that more and more part-time and tenure-ineli-
> gible faculty are being hired and that ever more classes
> are being taught by graduate students. . . . Our system of
> higher education is the best in the world, attracting thou-
> sand upon thousands of students from every corner of

the globe. We would do well not to undermine a basic
tenet that faculty require to exercise their freedoms in
research and teaching, unintimidated by intervention, inside or outside the university community.[41]

This is a typical justification for a system dating to the Middle Ages and widely instituted in this country half a century
ago. Yes, it's a shame that so many professors are unemployed
or underemployed. Yes, Raines seems to say, it's a shame that
so many professors make little use of their academic freedom. And yes, teaching is often undervalued at the expense
of arcane research. But the system has been in place for so
long, why change it?

Defenders of tenure are quick to point out that even granting the problems, the alternatives are worse. They may be
right. It is hard to know how much of the tapestry of academia would unravel if tenure were widely abolished or significantly altered. But most of the objections are based either on
what happened earlier in the century or on hypothetical pro-
jections of what might happen in the future. In the past few
years, more and more schools have moved away from absolute tenure, and some have eliminated tenure altogether.
Nearly 7 percent of colleges in the United States do not have
a tenure system.[42] What actually goes on in these places? Do
the dire prognostications of tenure absolutists come true? At
present, there simply isn't enough evidence one way or
another. It may be that at places like Bennington and New
College, academic freedom will disappear, consumerism will
dictate course offerings, and academics will be underpaid

and overworked. But only if these experiments are encouraged and carefully studied will we know. We could envision hundreds of variations on tenure, from its abolition in some places to a far easier granting of it at others. And it may be that variety would best meet the needs of a higher-education system that encompasses thousands of different schools. Tenure, at present, is a one-size-fits-all model, but at hundreds of colleges, it isn't the right size and it doesn't fit.

6

PROFESSORS AND SOCIETY

Debates over tenure expose the tension between academic culture and the society at large. Many professors feel some twangs of conscience about looking inward to the guild instead of outward to the community around them. But few feel able to attend to both the demands of scholarship and the needs of society. With such a large percentage of the population passing through the higher education system, the tug-of-war between professors and the larger society is all the more pressing. Academics rarely discuss the proper balance between their role as public servants and their allegiance to private guilds, and when they do, they hardly speak with one voice. Overall, they are divided over where their primary responsibility ought to lie and unsure to what degree their actions and attitudes should be guided by some notion of the public good.

The University of California at Berkeley is one of the premier research institutions in the world. Across the bay, right off the Pacific Ocean in the southwest corner of San Francisco, is another state school. San Francisco State University is part of the CalState system. Though its students are even more ethnically diverse than Berkeley's, they are also less affluent, and many put themselves through college.

Robert Cherny teaches history at San Francisco State, as he has for nearly three decades. When he was hired in 1968, SF State was a tie-dyed paradise, but even then, students and faculty saw themselves as the poor cousins of the more illustrious Berkeley. In part, that is an inevitable result of the California system. No state educates more college students than California, and no state is quite so rigorously tiered. The top tier, the University of California, is the research university. The CalState tier is meant primarily for teaching undergraduates for the B.A. While CalState schools grant M.A.'s, they don't offer the Ph.D., except in rare cases. The bottom tier is the community college system, which offers two-year associate's degrees and which is designed in part to prepare students to enter the other two tiers.

A specialist in late-nineteenth- and early-twentieth-century American history, Cherny is a bearded, balding man with a soft, deliberate voice. He met me during office hours, and our conversation was frequently interrupted by students seeking advice. Whenever a student would appear at his open door, Cherny would stop, invite them in, motion to me to turn off the tape recorder, and then turn his attention to the student. The contrast with star professors at Harvard, Yale, or Stanford could not have been greater.

Cherny cares deeply about teaching at a school where teaching is supposed to be the primary mission. Yet that doesn't mean he eschews research, and he gets slightly peeved when asked about the difference between being a professor at SF State and being a professor at Berkeley. "I've always felt that the distinction is an artificial one," he snapped. "I don't think that you can be an effective teacher unless you're actively involved in your field. There're different ways to be actively involved, but research is the key, and we expect our faculty to be involved in research. It's a false distinction that allows the legislature to give heavier teaching loads to State faculty than to UC faculty."

At Berkeley or UCLA, a professor typically teaches two courses a term. At the CalState level, however, a professor teaches at least three a term, and maybe more. Cherny has written several textbooks on his area of specialty, and he offered a long illustration of how his research in the archives enlivens his teaching in the classroom. He wants his students to think historically, to learn how to read documents from the period under study, how to analyze what is being said, and how to evaluate the accuracy of a particular piece of evidence.

Cherny believes that teaching enriches his research. "I've taught one lecture course on the history of the United States from the end of Reconstruction to World War I for twenty-five years, and each year it evolves and grows. You can never really know a subject unless you've had to teach it."

While most research universities do not place great emphasis on teaching when hiring or tenuring professors, SFSU does, at least in the history department. "We think of teaching as our first obligation," Cherny explained. "When we hire people we tell them that. When we hire people we ask for teaching evaluations to see how they've done. When we do tenure and promotion evaluations we look very carefully at teaching. It's required by the university, but different departments treat that in quite different ways on campus. Some departments only nod in that direction, and then emphasize research and grants. There are other departments that believe we should focus only on teaching. We in the history department fall somewhere in between."

California, like many states, has established a history requirement for undergraduates, and Cherny agrees that there is a civic purpose to history in general and to American history in particular. "In the California State system students are required to take six units of course work in U.S. history and three in state and local government. I've served on committees that approve courses to meet this requirement. So I'm familiar with the idea that there's a civic purpose, and I understand why legislatures take that position.

"But over time there may be a disparity between what legislatures or the regents require and what professors think about when they prepare these courses. What the California State Board of Trustees have in mind is that history is a social cement; it's what holds together a society, that you know your common past and by virtue of that are better able to function as a member of the society and take part in forming some kind of a common future. It gives people a sense of who they are by knowing where they come from.

"Of course, that's what the study of history does. Now whether it's a history that mindlessly glorifies patriotic myths, or whether it's a history that critically and analytically examines the past in an effort to understand what happened and why it happened, either way you're developing a common sense of where Americans came from and what their various group experiences or common experiences have been, and that gives you powerful ways of understanding where we are now. I think that the purpose of legislatures and trustees is compatible with what historians do if those historians think carefully about what the expectations of those legislatures and policy makers are."

Asked about whether historians do, in fact, "think carefully," Cherny rubbed his beard for several moments and said slowly, "Many of my colleagues do. Many of them think about what students need to know to understand themselves as American citizens."

It is true that many professors in the humanities think long and hard about the civic function of college in general and teaching in particular. Just as it is a rare individual who doesn't want to be liked by his or her students, it is a rare individual who doesn't need to believe that what he or she is doing has meaning. Most professors have an explanation for why they study what they study, even if it is nothing more complex than "I love it." Bob Cherny was most animated when discussing archives and documents. His passion is clearly for the Gilded Age, but that doesn't mean that he isn't a dedicated teacher.

As a group, most professors are indifferent about teaching. Both writing and teaching, however, are required of professors who are seeking tenure, and teaching is required of all professors, including those with tenure. Many academics find teaching painful and unpleasant. But whether they want to teach or not, they have to. Others are more comfortable in front of people, and still others actively enjoy teaching. Regardless of the comfort level, each professor comes up with some explanation, some rationale for teaching. The reason can be as simple as "I'm teaching because I have to teach in order to get a job as a professor and thereby have time to do the research I love." It's surprising just how many professors take this approach to their teaching, and it helps explain why students often feel that their professors are just going through the motions.

Still, many professors grapple with the goal of teaching. When they do, questions of the civic good arise. In the sciences, these questions can be answered on utilitarian grounds: Knowledge of science goes hand-in-hand with technological development, and the modern world depends on scientific innovation. But what is the use of the humanities?

Humanists prefer to reject questions of utility rather than answer them. Knowledge, they say, is important for its own sake. Any attempt to justify knowledge in terms of its social good undermines the purity of knowledge, undermines scholarship, and corrupts the primary purpose of academia and the university, which is to discover and preserve knowledge.

The preservation of knowledge—of history, literature, art, and culture—is clearly vital to the health and survival of a society. The artifacts of culture define who we are as surely as family pictures and memories of childhood. Without them, we are spiritually at a loss. But the preservation and articulation of humanistic knowledge could be accomplished by a few hundred institutions. We don't need 3,500 colleges and universities and hundreds of thousands of professors to perpetuate and develop knowledge.

Furthermore, teaching is not the same as preserving knowledge. Teaching is utilitarian. It is supposed to serve a function. Aware of that and uncomfortable with it, many professors have the most minimal expectations. For them, teaching means the transmission of knowledge from themselves to their students. The purpose of this transmission? Handing knowledge to the young is the only way to preserve it across time.

Nonacademics find this explanation incomprehensible. Students go to college for all sorts of reasons, but they aren't in the preservation business, and neither are parents, politicians, or the proverbial man on the street. State legislatures aren't allocating billions of dollars, the president isn't proposing tax credits for student loans, and parents aren't going into debt while their children are still fetuses in order for a few thousand professors to preserve knowledge. This isn't because Americans are anti-intellectual or philistine; it's because they know without necessarily thinking about it that the university and classroom education serve many civic functions, of which preservation is rarely the most important one.

In short, the primary way that academics identify the civic function of the university conflicts with the primary ways Americans outside the university identify the civic function. In fact, throughout a decade of conversations, classes, conferences, and reading, I have rarely heard humanities professors discuss what they do in terms of social utility or "the greater good." I have listened to and participated in intense and acrimonious debates about what certain groups in society expect of academia and why these groups are hostile to the pursuit of knowledge. The question of how academia and the humanities serve society almost never gets raised. No one asks what college is for.

Take the debates over tenure in Minnesota, Texas, and elsewhere. The tendency is for professors and academic guilds to see society—in the form of legislatures, students, and public interest groups—as a threat to intellectual freedom and to the academic endeavor. Society is perceived as a danger to be resisted, not a community to be served. Service need not mean capitulation to the demands of administrators or the ill-conceived plans of politicians, but it does carry with it a responsibility to engage and address the concerns of the world that surrounds the university, a world that the university is, whether academics like it or not, part of rather than separate from.

At a place like Harvard, with an endowment approaching $10 billion, with wealthy alumni and foundations stumbling over themselves to give money, and with a board of trustees elected privately by that community, professors are and should be free to do what they want. The same goes for most of the Ivy League schools and for dozens of small, elite, liberal arts schools. As long as they have the money—the private money—to fund their activities, these places can claim the right of any private institution in a free society and choose their priorities as they see fit. If Harvard faculty want to study the most arcane knowledge and preserve it, and if such study costs $10 million a year, and if the university administrators are willing to allocate the funds, and parents continue sending their kids, and alumni and foundations keep giving money, then the Harvard faculty can be as arcane or as relevant as they see fit.

Delving into the obscure and uncovering the hidden serve the public good of preserving knowledge, but as long as there is a Harvard, and a Princeton, Stanford, Chicago, Yale, and so on, capable of setting their priorities in this way and then paying for them, society's need for knowledge will be fulfilled.

That leaves the other 90-plus percent of higher education in the United States, including the public sphere, where more than 80 percent of students now go and where the bulk of money is now spent.

Even here, if each state wants to create a few select campuses that have knowledge preservation and articulation as the primary goals, then a public good is served by a Berkeley, an Austin, a Madison, an Ann Arbor, or a Stony Brook. Academic guilds and professional organizations act as if every place ought to aspire to become a Harvard, a Berkeley, a Yale, and that anything else falls short. That vision clashes with the public good and damages society. It represents a profound and disturbing inability of academics to see their civic function.

At the same time, there's a difference between how academic guilds identify themselves and how individual professors or graduate students identify themselves. While "Americans" might define themselves as citizens of a country devoted to free expression and the free market, individual Americans don't necessarily define themselves in the same way. While the guilds are mostly silent about the civic purpose of the humanities, individual professors like Bob Cherny do think about the public good. Yet even at an individual level, professors conceive of their role in society differently from the way many of the people and institutions paying their bills do.

I asked the following question of professors at public colleges: "Do you see yourself primarily as a member of the college faculty, as a member of an academic guild, or as a public servant of the state?" Almost everyone I talked to answered that their primary allegiance is to the guild and then to the college they teach at. Most reacted with some confusion or skepticism to the notion that they might be public servants. That is hardly surprising, given the culture of academia. The focus of the academic career is one's scholarly peers. American historians write for other American historians; deconstructionists for other deconstructionists. They do not write for their colleagues in other departments in buildings across from theirs at the same college, and they don't write for the public.

Sometimes, they write for their students. Classes require textbooks, and textbooks require authors. The entire college population constitutes a market for textbooks, and professors frequently augment their income writing texts. But texts are never seen as "real" scholarship or as tenurable knowledge. An assistant professor who writes a text on nineteenth-century American poetry may earn a nice supplement to her salary, but she will earn no professional benefit when it comes to her promotion. That is because textbooks are utilitarian rather than scholarly, and scholarship is *the* criterion for advancement in the guild. Textbooks require synthesis and simplification, where scholarship requires original research and original thought. Scholarship, in other words, is shorthand for the preservation and articulation of knowledge.

Given the structure of professional advancement, it's not surprising that professors see themselves as members of a guild above all else. The guild evaluates your work, the guild makes your reputation, and the guild determines your success. If the guild doesn't give high marks to your scholarship, then your department is unlikely to promote you. In a very real way, therefore, the community of scholars in your field has more power and more influence over your career than administrators at the college that employs you and colleagues in the department you belong to.

This leads to a peculiar form of identification. "I have more in common with scholars in my field who teach in Japan than I do with professors across the hall," remarked one distinguished Harvard political scientist. "I E-mail Japan several times a week, but I might not speak to colleagues in other disciplines more than a few times in a decade." This type of identification suits the scholarly endeavor. It does not suit the needs of American higher education, which serves more than 15 million students.

Professors have always had an ambivalent relationship with the world outside of the university. As we have seen, they prefer detachment from the political and social currents that swirl around the ivory tower. Sometimes, that disengage-

known as "public scholarship." Like its cousin "public journalism," public scholarship is an attempt to match research
with public interests and issues. In part, public scholarship
simply implies a change in attitude and priorities. Rather
than attending purely to the guild, the public scholar assesses
how scholars might serve the culture. For example, rather
than teaching several courses on the Gilded Age, a professor
like Bob Cherny might teach a course on the history of public housing. According to Jay Rosen, a leading proponent of
both public scholarship and public journalism who teaches at
NYU, "Public scholars begin with the realization that they
don't know something, and that something can be known in
only one way: through a process of inquiry conducted with
others in public."[5] Thus, the public scholar uses a broader
range of research tools. The public historian must rely not
just on archives and works by other scholars but on the con-
tributions of journalists, politicians, schoolteachers, heads of
local historical societies, and other informed citizens. Public
history tries to provide historical studies geared to the needs
of the surrounding community. Public historians work not
just in the university but at libraries, historical societies, and
museums.[6]

Not surprisingly, public scholarship has many critics in
academe. Some are uncomfortable with a research and
teaching agenda that risks being determined by the public
passions of the moment, and many academics wonder how
substantive public scholarship can be if the questions asked
and the audience addressed are not scholarly. Whether one
appreciates public scholarship, the debate itself leads aca-

demics to think more about what they are doing and why. This debate must be expanded.[7]

Joyce Appleby, the 1997 president of the American Historical Association, set up an informal "op-ed" service, which connects professors with newspaper and magazine editors in order to facilitate informed commentary on pressing news issues. Appleby recognized that most professors write in a style that is unappealing to the general reading public. As a result, editors for commercial publications are often wary of soliciting academics. By encouraging professors to apply their scholarly knowledge to current events, Appleby hoped to narrow the gulf separating academia from society.

Yet Appleby still draws a firm distinction between writing for newspapers and writing for scholarly journals and an audience of one's academic peers. On the one hand, she is a strong advocate of scholars serving the larger community. In her words, the role of the AHA is "to create the means for historians, not just in universities, but also those working in museums and public institutions, to make an impact on public issues that affect history, history education, and history scholarship. I also think it's very important to bring to the public the knowledge that historians have."

This was one reason why she set up the op-ed service. But when I asked her whether writing opinion pieces ought to count toward professional advancement, she didn't hesitate before dismissing the idea. "It's not scholarship," she replied.

I asked why not.

"Because it isn't," she answered. "It's using knowledge and opinions that you have and applying them to an issue. Spend-

ing five hours writing an op-ed piece isn't equivalent to
spending four or five months writing a scholarly article, writing something that's a good deal more demanding. We teach
and we research. That's the substance of the profession, not
journalism. I resist the idea that we're going to fold everything into our profession. Otherwise you get creeping total-
ization of a person's life. I don't like this expansion of the
profession to embrace activities that aren't part of the intellectual or academic experience."

"Then where does writing for newspapers fit into a professor's life," I asked.

"Everybody has some free time," she said. "They can play
racquetball or write an op-ed piece."

Those who devote their time to writing for the general
public rather than plowing the fields of scholarship are often
harshly criticized by their peers. While academic luminaries
such as Harvard's Henry Louis Gates and Robert Coles, Columbia's Simon Schama and Edward Said, or Princeton's
Sean Wilentz are familiar fixtures in the pages of magazines
and newspapers, they elicit as much derision as respect from
their academic colleagues. Because their high public profile
puts the university's name in the spotlight, university administrators support their nonscholarly endeavors, and the
salaries of star public professors often exceed those of their
less visible peers.[8]

Professors who write for the popular press are sometimes
referred to as "public intellectuals." The preponderance of
academics detest the term, including some of those saddled
with it. Dozens of academics at that Chicago conference rose

to express their dislike and distrust of any intellectual who seeks a commercial audience. Two factors account for this attitude. One has been mentioned, and that is the feeling among academics that too much interaction with the world outside contaminates the purity of scholarship. The other is a leftist critique of the market. In the sixties and seventies, the university was seen by many professors as an accomplice to the state. Perceived as an ally of the same forces that waged war in Vietnam and broke into the Watergate complex, the university was attacked by students and professors in demonstration after demonstration.

Today, however, the university is seen by these same left-leaning professors as the last sanctuary for ideas. Only in the university, this reasoning goes, can ideas that have no commercial appeal flourish. That includes both obscure ideas and controversial ones. Commercial publishing, controlled by multimedia conglomerates, is seen as a haven only for safe ideas or for perspectives that support the free market. Therefore, because they associate with the market, "public intellectuals" sacrifice integrity in return for money and fame. They become not public but "puppet" intellectuals.[9]

Appleby noted that writing for the general public could constitute "community service," that inchoate category in tenure evaluations that tends to receive even less weight than teaching. Some professors feel that community service, like teaching, is more important to society than research, and they believe that professors should think seriously about shifting their priorities. But community service has its critics as well. "My university," wrote Father John Piderit, the president of

Loyola University in Chicago, "has a new Center for Urban Research and Learning that is forming partnerships with community organizations to address major issues facing cities. . . . Yet this kind of community involvement, however important, should not be allowed to substitute for a university's primary mission, which is to serve students."[10]

And then there are those who believe that contemporary scholarship is integrally connected to the larger society. Just as doctors delve into highly specialized research in order to prolong life and improve health, so too scholars spend years probing what may seem to be obscure topics for the greater good of society.[11] Decades ago, goes this thinking, academic research suffered from genuine irrelevance, but the topics pursued by scholars in the humanities today are closely linked to questions of cultural identity, race, gender, ideas of nation, attitudes toward other countries, and a range of issues that animate our public life. It's unfortunate that academic jargon obscures so much of academic writing and makes it inaccessible. Strip away the jargon, and we would find a rich body of literature and research that bears directly on the social and political conundrums of society.

These jumbled debates over the proper relationship between the professor and society show no signs of sorting themselves out anytime soon. For much of the century, academics have argued over whether the primary mission of the university ought to be teaching or research.[12] The dispute over the relative merits of being a "public intellectual" has lasted at least thirty years. And there still is no consensus about the appropriate amount of community service for a professor or a university. Once again, however, the demographic changes in higher education and the explosion of public financing for it means that these debates now matter for society as a whole. In short, these debates are no longer academic.

It's striking how little room there is in these debates for multiple identities. In a system that encompasses more than three thousand campuses, hundreds of thousands of professors, and millions of graduate and undergraduate students, there is bound to be immense variety. Yet academics argue as if only one identity were appropriate: "We should be scholars!" "No, we should be classroom teachers!" "On the contrary, we have a responsibility to serve the local community!" "No, the nation!" "No, no, we should be popular writers!" "Actually, we have a duty to transform the world, speak truth to power, and challenge prejudice!" "In the end, what matters most is knowledge."

Why is this debate framed in absolute terms? Why should the identity of so many people roughly engaged in something called higher education be reduced to one primary function? Instead of either/or, why not all? Who said that American higher education is not a system where a thousand flowers might bloom?

In reality, they do. The tens of thousands of adjuncts at community colleges are teachers, under deplorable labor conditions, but teachers, first and last. They aren't expected to research, and they wouldn't have the time if they were. At places like San Francisco State, teaching is at least as important for one's professional advancement as scholarship. And at small liberal arts colleges, one's "fit" with other colleagues and popularity with students loom large in hiring and tenuring decisions. At the Ivy League schools and the premier state campuses, research is king, grant money a sign of success, and publications the mark of productivity.

But while the reality is one of multiplicity, the ideal is still the scholar. The debates are framed in reference to that unitary ideal. In law, it would be as if all lawyers aspired to be litigators at Wall Street firms. That would leave an immense gap in a society that needs public defenders, prosecutors, and general service lawyers in towns and counties throughout the country. Imagine if all of those local lawyers brokering land deals, divorces, and wills were simultaneously trying to write articles for the *Harvard Law Review*. Imagine that the American Bar Association said that, yes, wills are important, but the real work of lawyers is corporate litigation on Wall Street. That would create inconceivable problems within the legal profession and within American society, and though many of us might rejoice to see lawyers thrown into turmoil, it would ultimately harm all of us.

In academia, the mold of the scholar now does more harm than good. It not only excludes other valuable professional identities, but it also fits an increasingly small number of universities and professors. It is a mold that still makes sense at perhaps a few hundred colleges and universities in the United States. And even there, it is constrictive. Some professors break the mold. They become "public intellectuals" or community activists. They devote their attention to teaching and to their students. They become involved in political movements or university governance. In short, they do what they want, whether it is going about their responsibilities in a desultory fashion or taking up gardening to fill their time outside the six hours a week, six months a year they have to be in a classroom. And some feel a strong responsibility to apply their knowledge to "the public good."

When professors approach a public issue, they can be immensely helpful. They provide historical, cultural, and analytic perspectives that are often missing in politics and journalism. But they can also be startlingly at odds with the larger culture they are trying to serve. After decades spent within the academy, professors sometimes emerge into society with a set of ideas about what constitutes the public good that seem perfectly reasonable within the academy but are utterly incomprehensible and even reprehensible to the rest of society.

One of the most striking examples of the clash between the academy and the larger society over what constitutes the public good was the controversy surrounding national history standards. With the best of intentions, a distinguished group of professors led a multiyear effort to determine what history all American schoolkids should be taught. The standards were published in 1994 and immediately denounced by centrist and conservative pundits and by most of the United States Senate. To the surprise and dismay of the professors who created the standards, people outside the university have their own definition of history. In the university, professors and professors alone determine history, but in society, they are only one voice. In the public square, others speak, more loudly, more fluently, and more effectively. The national history standards showed how detached professors can be. The controversy exposed the insensitivity of academics to the cultural currents that swirl around the ivory tower, and it showed that in the tug-of-war to define American identity, groups within the larger society will fight professors by fair means and foul.

7

HISTORY
STANDARDS

In the early 1980s, the achievement levels of American schoolchildren fell behind those of schoolchildren in other developed nations. Judging from test scores in everything from math to history, American students compared unfavorably to students in France, Germany, Japan, Korea, and elsewhere. This raised concerns that the United States would not be able to maintain its competitive edge in a world increasingly dominated by information, technology, and service industries. Politicians took up the call for improved performance, and many felt that what the United States lacked was a set of national performance standards.[1]

At the September 1989 meeting of the National Governors Association, George Bush announced an initiative for standards in the schools. "The time has come," he said, "to establish clear national performance goals, goals that will make us internationally competitive and second to none in the twenty-first century."[2] He called for a national initiative to design standards in all major subjects. One of the most ar-

dent gubernatorial supporters was Governor Bill Clinton of
Arkansas, and in the spring of 1994, after years of wrangling
over the exact language, Congress authorized a program
known as Goals 2000.

In addition to calling for a reduction in the high school
dropout rates and a more active role for parents in their children's education, Goals 2000 mandated that "by the year
2000, all students will leave grades 4, 8, and 12 having
demonstrated competency over challenging subject matter
including English, mathematics, science, foreign languages,
civics and government, economics, arts, history, and geography, and every school in America will ensure that all students
learn to use their minds well, so they may be prepared for responsible citizenship, further learning, and productive employment in our Nation's modern economy."[3]

As this legislation made its way through Congress in the
early 1990s, several groups of university professors, education specialists, and schoolteachers began to work on standards in a number of areas, including English, math, civics,
and history. These groups were independent associations, not
government commissions, and funding came from both public and private sources. One of these sources was the National
Endowment for the Humanities, which from 1986 to 1992
was chaired by Lynne Cheney.

Cheney was a vocal champion of education reform and a for-
midable presence in Washington. The wife of Richard Cheney,
a Republican congressman until 1988 and then Bush's secretary of defense until 1992, Lynne Cheney was a prominent
critic of multiculturalism and a strong advocate of "traditional

values." Along with former secretary of education William Bennett, Cheney was in the vanguard of the conservative cultural critics who assailed what they saw as a pernicious relativism and "blame America first" stance that dominated all levels of humanistic education in the United States.

The search for standards transcended party lines and ideologies, but it was still something of a surprise when in December 1991 Cheney agreed to grant more than half a million dollars to the National Center for History in the Schools, based at the University of California at Los Angeles. That grant was matched by nearly $900,000 from the Department of Education. The NEH had funded the center since 1988 in order "to support an integrated program of research, development, and national dissemination to improve the teaching of history in the nation's schools."[4] But the new grant was for something more specific, and something unprecedented—national standards for history.

The director of the center was Charlotte Crabtree, a professor of education. Though her sympathies are with the left, Crabtree excelled at consensus building, and she managed to win the trust of people at opposite ends of the political spectrum. She was praised by Cheney as "very intelligent and very patient," yet she also earned the respect of the most radical teachers and professors. The codirector of the new standards project was a UCLA professor of history, Gary Nash. Heading up what was now called the National History Standards Project, Crabtree and Nash assembled a national council to oversee the project. Nearly thirty distinguished professors and educators were appointed to the council, a number of them on Cheney's recommendation. Along with the council, Crabtree and Nash set up a national forum composed of representatives from two dozen interested associations. Nine major professional organizations, including the American Historical Association, the Organization of American Historians, the Organization of History Teachers, and the National Council for Social Studies, agreed to act as focus groups, and over the next two years, these groups provided detailed critiques of the various drafts. Finally, Nash and Crabtree created curriculum committees for U.S. and world history standards. These committees, which were composed almost entirely of high school teachers from across the country, did most of the actual writing of the standards.

For the first six months, the project hammered out the criteria for the standards. Central to the endeavor was the notion that history is an essential component of civic virtue. That wasn't exactly a controversial stance. American political leaders, educators, and assorted cultural literati have always stressed the vital importance of history in American society. For generations, Americans of various stripes have said that a coherent national identity depends on teaching children a common narrative of the American past.

Though it took months of rewrites and revisions before all groups were satisfied with the language, the final criteria reflected this perspective. "The reasons [to study history] are many, but none are more important to a democratic society than this: *knowledge of history is the precondition of political intelligence*. . . . Standards in United States history should contribute to citizenship education through developing understanding of our common civic identity and shared civic values. . . ."[5]

The next two and a half years were marked by a number of internal disputes. One involved the wording for the criterion that would guide the world history standards. According to the initial draft in the spring of 1992, "Standards in world history should include both the history and values of western civilization and the history and culture of other societies, with the greater emphasis on western civilization, and on the interrelationships between western and nonwestern societies."[6]

This language set off a long and bitter debate between various groups involved in the standards. The American Historical Association, represented by its director and a group of historians assembled as part of the AHA focus group, refused to endorse any set of standards that emphasized "Western civilization" more than other cultures. The eminent Chicago historian William McNeill insisted that Western civilization didn't deserve greater emphasis than other major civilizations. "The west is not privileged," he wrote, "indeed we are a minority in the world and ought to know it." Others disagreed and believed firmly that Western civilization should be at the center of any world history curriculum in the United States.[7] Eventually, a compromise was reached, and the final wording stated that "Standards in world history should treat the history and values of diverse civilizations, including those of the West, and should especially address the interactions among them."

Another fissure was whether the standards would emphasize process or content. This was a debate primarily between schoolteachers and education specialists on the one hand and professional historians on the other. Many of the education specialists felt that rather than place so much weight on details, the standards ought to focus on "civic virtue" and "critical analysis."[8] In the end, the standards established guidelines for both historical thinking (process) and historical events (content). But the emphasis was clearly on content, and that reflected the bias of the professors.

Less evident, but ultimately more consequential, was the problem of political ideology. The OAH, noted one member of the council, was composed of historians "divided politically between Center and Left, while the country is split among Center, Left and Right." This member feared that the professors involved in the project would not take sufficient care to propose standards that represented compromise on all sides. His concern would prove prophetic.[9]

Looking back on the two years it took to draw up the standards, Gary Nash felt that a good balance had been struck between left and right, between those who wanted mostly process and those who wanted mostly content. Nash is a veteran of curriculum debates, and before becoming the co-director of the standards project, he had authored a number of school textbooks and helped write standards for the state of California. Nash is nothing if not laid-back. He speaks deliberately, in a rich baritone voice, and he lives in a pleasant house with southwestern decor right off the ocean just south of Malibu.

"Our goal," he began, "was to create high standards reflecting the best scholarship of the last several generations.

The point was to inspire teachers, as well as publishers, and to influence the people who produce teachers in the schools of education, schools that teach pedagogy but not a lot of content." Contrary to the concerns raised by the OAH representative, Nash was proud of the fact that the national council and the forum brought together people from across the ideological spectrum, and as the process drew toward completion in the summer of 1994, both he and Crabtree were confident that they had overseen an endeavor that would be remembered for decades to come. "My view was that those history standards will be looked upon as the most important and the most extensive collaboration ever between people in different levels of our educational hierarchy."

As it turned out, the standards probably will be remembered, but not necessarily for the reasons that Nash touted. Just prior to publication, Nash sat down with Cheney's successor at the NEH, Sheldon Hackney. Hackney wanted to know what to expect when the standards were issued, and he especially wanted to be forewarned of possible controversies. Nash told Hackney that if there was going to be any fire, it would come in response to the world history standards, which were still considered by some members of the committee to be insufficiently multicultural. As for the American history standards, Nash wasn't worried. The council had been unanimous in its praise for the standards, and even the more conservative historians had endorsed them.

During the vetting period that preceded publication, a sour note was struck by Chester Finn, a former assistant secretary of education in the Reagan administration whose Education

Excellence Network refused to endorse the final version of the standards. Finn had been critical from the beginning of the process, and he warned that if the standards didn't fly with "Joe Six Pack in Omaha," then they weren't going to fly with the American public in general. Finn felt that from the outset, the way that the historians and schoolteachers were conceiving of the standards ensured that "Joe Six Pack" would be turned off.[10] With his feet firmly planted in the conservative camp, Finn believed that the academic elite were not only out of touch with the American people but subversively opposed to the cherished myths and values of the American public.

Almost without exception, the members of the forum and the council rejected Finn's critique. According to Nash, Finn was so far apart from the rest of the group that people who had been happy to argue with each other over the standards realized that their differences weren't nearly as great as their differences with Finn. They may have disagreed with each other over various points of interpretation and emphasis, but they all opposed Finn. When the U.S. history standards were published in the fall of 1994, however, editorial pages throughout the country were filled with outraged reactions that echoed Finn's criticisms. The voices that had been in such a minority throughout the two-year process proved to be a majority in the media and in the halls of Congress.

The first shot was fired by Lynne Cheney herself. In an editorial published in *The Wall Street Journal* on October 20, 1994, Cheney decried the standards: "Imagine an outline for the teaching of American history in which George Washington makes only a fleeting appearance and is never described as our first president. Or in which the founding of the Sierra Club and the National Organization for Women are considered noteworthy events, but the first gathering of the U.S. Congress is not." She continued her attack by claiming that "not a single one of the 31 standards mentions the Constitution." She was particularly upset because as NEH chairman she had funded the UCLA Center that oversaw the project, but she claimed that standards were shaped by a 1992 presidential election "that unleashed the forces of political correctness" and that allowed the historians on the project to give full vent to their "hatred for traditional history." She concluded by urging people to reject the standards: "We are a better people than the National Standards indicate, and our children deserve to know it."

Cheney's preemptive cultural strike led to a media storm. Nash and Cheney made the rounds on the talk-show circuit, appearing on PBS's *McNeil-Lehrer Report*, on ABC News, and on the *Today* show. On *Good Morning, America*, Cheney said that the problem with the standards wasn't what was in them but what was missing. On top of that, she objected to the animus toward hero worship that she believed permeated the standards. "I think our kids need heroes," she told Charles Gibson, the show's host. "I think that they need models of greatness to help them aspire. I think they need heroes so that they can become heroes themselves."[11]

Cheney found a ready ally in Rush Limbaugh. On his television and radio broadcasts at the end of October, Limbaugh ridiculed the standards and Gary Nash. "Let me tell you something, folks. History is real simple. You know what history is? It's what happened. It's no more—don't applaud that. . . . I mean, that's one of the cheapest applause lines there is. Now the problem you get into is when guys like [Nash] try to skew history by, 'Well, let's interpret what happened because maybe we don't find the truth in the facts, or at least we don't like the truth as it's presented. So let's change the interpretation a little bit so that it will be the way we wished it were.' Well, that's not what history is." Limbaugh then listed people he claimed were not in the standards, people like Paul Revere, Robert E. Lee, and George Washington. He said that everyone needs heroes. "Heroes point to what's possible," Limbaugh stated. But multiculturalists opposed the notion of hero worship. "If this stuff grabs hold," he warned, America will no longer be a strong society.[12]

After Limbaugh disseminated Cheney's critique to his millions of listeners, there was a further round of newspaper and magazine articles. In his column in the *Washington Post*, the curmudgeonly conservative Charles Krauthammer went one step further. He claimed that the standards had been "hijacked by the educational establishment and turned into a classic of political correctness." Krauthammer singled out Nash as the main culprit: "Nash, it seems, was bored by the fact-based history of his childhood." Rather than events and facts, the standards presented an ethnic smorgasbord of opinions and counternarratives that painted American history in the most hostile terms imaginable.[13] Throughout the country, conservative columnists and radio talk-show hosts had the standards squarely in their sights. They dismissed the standards as a document produced by refugees from the 1960s and "riddled with propaganda."[14] Others accused the historians of imposing their own values on a country that did not share them.[15]

Defenders of the standards were given the opportunity to respond, and they did their best to rebut the criticisms. Writing in the *Los Angeles Times*, Professor Ruth Rosen warned that certain right-wing ideologues were attempting to dictate the way the past is understood. If they succeeded, the result would be an Orwellian society in which those "who control the past, control the future."[16] In the *New York Times*, Carol Gluck, a professor at Columbia University who was a member of the national council, rebutted the idea that the standards were hijacked. The process was an unusually open one, she claimed, with more than six thousand teachers, professors, and educators adding their perspectives.[17] The *San Francisco Chronicle* took an editorial stance against Cheney and the assorted critics: "The thinking-person's approach to teaching and inclusion of long-ignored groups makes the document an essential and important starting point for a revolution in U.S. history instruction."[18] Professional historians were for the most part supportive and concerned. The executive secretary of the Organization of American Historians worried that the debate over the standards, shaped as it was by Cheney, Limbaugh, and the like, "threatens to create a serious misunderstanding, if not demonization, of several decades of scholarship in American history."[19]

In Washington, however, the critics found a welcome audience in the Republican Party. Having captured both the Senate and the House of Representatives in the midterm elections of 1994, the "Republican Revolution" swept into Washington in January 1995, and one of the first things the newly ascendant Republicans did was condemn the national history standards developed at UCLA. Both the world history and U.S. history manuals were denounced, but throughout these debates, it was the U.S. history standards that really irked the Republicans. One of the items of the Republican agenda was to defund both the National Endowment for the Arts and the National Endowment for the Humanities. In years past, the right had attacked the NEA by pointing to the art of Andres Serrano and to the photographs of Robert Mapplethorpe. According to these critics, by funding Serrano and Mapplethorpe the NEA showed how little it respected mainstream American values.

Just as the homoerotic works of Mapplethorpe were used to assail the NEA, the national history standards were used to attack the NEH. Cheney was one of the leading proponents of defunding the NEH, and she used the standards as a weapon against the agency she once led.[20] In January, as the Republican-controlled Congress assembled in Washington, Senator Slade Gorton, Republican from Washington, portrayed the standards as a national scandal. At the start of a very heady Gingrich revolution, the attention of the Senate turned not to the vast changes promised by the Contract with America but instead to a seemingly innocuous set of guidelines for voluntary history standards.

Speaking to the Senate on January 18, Gorton bluntly stated that "this set of standards must be stopped, abolished, repudiated, repealed. It must be recalled like a shipload of badly contaminated food. . . . In order to stop this perverted idea in its tracks, and to ensure that it docs not become, de facto, a guide for our Nation's classrooms, it must be publicly and officially repudiated by this Congress."

In order to accomplish that, Gorton introduced an amendment that would have denied federal funding to agencies and groups that endorsed the standards. Senate Democrats looked for some way to prevent the amendment from being passed. They succeeded, but the victory was Pyrrhic. Gorton agreed to present his platform as a "sense-of-the-Senate" resolution, which wouldn't have the binding force of an amendment. In return, the Democrats agreed to vote in favor of the resolution. And that is precisely what they did. By a vote of 99 to 1, the United States Senate declared that any voluntary standards called for by Goals 2000 "should not be based on standards developed by the National Center for History in the Schools." In the future, the resolution concluded, anyone developing such standards "should have a decent respect for United States' history's roots in western civilization."[21]

The Senate condemnation earned plaudits from the columnists and commentators who had earlier attacked the standards.[22] But there was also a good deal of criticism of the Senate for making such a heavy-handed foray into cultural matters.[23] Faculty at universities throughout the country wrote letters to their state representatives decrying the Senate vote. Mark Leff, an associate professor at the University of Illinois at Urbana-Champaign, appealed to Senator Carol Moseley-Braun not to let the resolution stand unchallenged. "I'm truly worried," Leff wrote, "about the chilling effect that recent attacks have had."[24] Other historians had a more ambivalent reaction. Arthur Schlesinger, one of the deans of modern American history, told Nash that while he rejected "Cheney-type attacks," he had reservations about the standards themselves. Nash responded defensively to Schlesinger's critique, but he acknowledged that there were areas where the standards could be improved.[25]

In order to mollify critics like Schlesinger, the national council published a revised version of the standards in the spring of 1996. There was some change in emphasis, but the most substantial revision was really an excision. The teaching examples, which had attracted the majority of attention, were removed and published as a supplement. These new standards received far less media scrutiny. They were endorsed by Schlesinger and Diane Ravitch in the *Wall Street Journal*,[26] but many remained skeptical.[27] By the time the revised edition came out, the mainstream media had already moved on to other issues.

Looking back at the controversy, Gary Nash admitted that while the road had been rougher than he had anticipated, he was pleased with the ultimate outcome. "We're winning this war big-time," he said with some pride. "We're just thrashing the hell out of them. We may have lost the first inning, but it's a nine-inning game. They're way ahead in the media war, but they're far behind in terms of what teachers think and in terms of how much attention they pay to this firestorm."

A battle had ended with both sides triumphantly declaring victory. The only apparent combatants had been conservative politicians and cultural critics on one side, and professors along with schoolteachers and some liberal journalists and politicians on the other. Each side claimed to be speaking for the American people, and if one were to judge the outcome based on media coverage and senatorial debates, then clearly the conservatives achieved their goals. But Nash, Crabtree, Joyce Appleby, and other historians asserted that politicians in Washington and columnists for the predominantly northeastern media spoke only for themselves, not for America.

The history standards debate exposed a deep fissure between academia and those who control politics and the media.[28] Talking to people on both sides, I realized that for some, the culture wars of the late 1980s and early 1990s are alive and well.[29] For those involved in the history standards debate, the battle rages on. Nash spoke of winning the war; Cheney and Limbaugh said much the same, and Senator Gorton must have felt victorious when he maneuvered ultraliberal senators like Paul Wellstone into voting against a multicultural set of standards. In the fray, most people lost sight of what the standards actually said, though it's unlikely that many of the people who took a position for or against had even read the three volumes. Like *The Satanic Verses*, the national history standards could only be used as a symbol if much of what they actually said was ignored.

The books themselves consisted of dozens of general standards and hundreds of pages of very specific teaching examples. In fact, the standard books contained more facts and information than any teacher could possibly digest or utilize in the course of the school year. The process behind the standards guaranteed information overload. Nash and Crabtree, as well as Ross Dunn on the world history side, wanted the process to be democratic, inclusive, and equitable. They also wanted to make sure that the high school teachers and the education specialists felt like partners and not second-class citizens. Therefore, they incorporated just about anything that someone on the council, forum, or focus groups considered important.

One focus group would review a draft chapter on the Civil War and suggest that more examples of African Americans be incorporated. So they were. Another group would suggest that the strategies of Grant and Sherman be included. So they were. Yet another would say that students should be encouraged to read historical fiction. And that too was added. The end result should have been criticized for offering too much too indiscriminately rather than for presenting too little "traditional history." Cheney and Slade Gorton not only distorted the contents of the standards; they lied about what had and had not been omitted. Again, it's doubtful that many of the critics actually read the text, and Gorton probably didn't care whether his representation of the details was accurate so much as he saw an opportunity to rally the cultural conservatives.

Cheney, however, knew what the standards said, and so she knew that George Washington and the Constitution were not left out. They were not included in the main headings, because these were written in general terms. For instance, Standard 1 of Era 3 (Revolution and the New Nation) read: "Students Should Understand: The causes of the American Revolution, the ideas and interests involved in forging the revolutionary movement, and the reasons for the American victory." Standard 3 said: "Students Should Understand: The institutions and practices of government created during the revolution and how they were revised between 1787 and 1815 to create the foundation of the American political system." Attached to these general standards were pages of teaching examples, which specifically mentioned the Constitution, Thomas Jefferson, George Washington, and other "heroes" multiple times.

The sheer mass of text made the standards seem undifferentiated, and that enabled Cheney and other critics to misrepresent them. By presenting so many different factors as if they were of equal importance, the standards could be impugned for failing to draw attention to what was really important. Defenders of the standards insisted that all of the traditional heroes and events were included, but they missed the point of the conservative attack. For many Americans, history *is* the story of heroes and cherished myths. For many Americans, history is an affirmative epic of how we became who we are. And for all their inclusiveness, the standards simply do not approach history as a compendium of morally uplifting parables.

It isn't just conservatives who think of history this way. According to a *Newsweek* article on the purpose of history, "Americans are born, and then they are made. Tradition has it that history teachers have been anointed with the crucial task of infusing our country's facts—and myths—into its youngest most malleable citizens."[30] Many Americans see history education as the most "civic" subject, and they view history as one of the few binding forces in an otherwise divided society. For them, history has a purpose, and it should be taught in order to best serve that purpose. The purpose isn't self-knowledge or critical thinking. It's unity; it's national identity; it's a grounding in a common past so that we can approach the present together.

Historians don't see history this way. In fact, they tend to believe that this vision of history is wrong. And not only wrong but dangerous. History for historians is not a binding force or a set of uplifting stories meant to glue America together. History is not composed of heroes and great deeds. Historians interpret history through the lens of academia as a series of problems and questions, as a puzzle with missing pieces, and as morally neutral. History for most Americans has a civic purpose; history for most historians is a discipline.

The two aren't necessarily exclusive, but in the process of drawing up the standards, the historians who designed the project approached history as their professional training dictated. As we've seen, that training conditions professors to focus on questions valued by their guilds. At times, guild concerns may converge with societal concerns, but even when they do, academics come up with "academic" responses.

That is precisely what happened with the national history standards. The project began as a societal issue. Two presidents, George Bush and Bill Clinton, as well as successive governors' conferences, stressed the need for standards in education. Responding to the call for standards, professors in different subjects organized projects, and one of these was the National History Standards Project. Two federal agencies granted this project a million and a half dollars because the issue of standards was a high priority in Washington and in state capitals throughout the country. The federal agencies believed that the point of standards was to raise the level of primary and secondary education in the United States so that Americans would be able to continue to compete in a competitive international market. The historians who requested the money and who headed the project believed that the point of standards was, according to Gary Nash, "to create high standards reflecting the best scholarship of the last several generations."

From the outset, the motives of the politicians and bureaucrats were different from the motives of the historians. Yet these motives were not implicitly incompatible. The historians might have satisfied both ambitions, but they did not. Why? Because it never occurred to them that theirs was not the only agenda.

Professor Morton Keller was a member of the national council. He's a charming man, retired after years of teaching at Brandeis University, in Waltham, Massachusetts, and he now spends his days researching a book he plans to write on the history of Harvard. But when he recounts his experiences on the history standards project, his eyes darken and his voice becomes heavier. Like Nash, he was concerned about incorporating the best scholarship: "The point initially wasn't to develop or impose a uniform curriculum on the land but to produce something that would reflect the current state of American history in ways that would make it meaningful and useful to students and teachers. I didn't think there was a sharply focused ideological agenda. There were tensions between those who were more political and those who were less, but the debates were more over nuance. No deep and profound clashes." He paused and said almost apologetically, "I wanted to bring together new historiography and make it available to teachers."

The vociferous response from the right surprised and dismayed Keller. "The reaction did jolt me. I think I'd gotten too much into the internal workings of the process to see the perspectives of people with a civics agenda like Cheney and even the original governors' conference. But balancing that agenda with ours was never really considered.

"The fact is that the prevailing attitudes about a lot of these issues in the historical profession are very far indeed from the prevailing attitudes of the society at large. But I hope that the engagement between academia and society will eventually take the form of a mutual learning experience. Some of the critics will have to learn that there really is more to American history than what they learned in their civics textbooks. And some of the historians have to learn that you have to have a decent respect for the opinions of mankind.

"The most effective criticism of the standards, in retrospect, is not what they left out or kept in but that we weren't sufficiently sensitive about how they would be perceived by the consumer. After all, this wasn't a paper commissioned to be read at the American Historical Association. The standards struck like a pail full of cold water in the face of the public at large. These were something that were going to go out into the public arena, and you have to be political if you're going to go into that. History is not like mathematics, not a series of agreed-upon formulations. We have to have a decent respect for the opinions of the consumers."

Much of that larger society couldn't have cared less about the standards. Any pressing issue has interest groups. Outside of those groups, not many people actively pay attention. The destruction of the rain forest in the Olympia Peninsula in Washington galvanizes the Sierra Club, logging companies, the Department of the Interior, and some members of Congress. But there are far more Americans who don't know or don't care about the trees of the Northwest. So too with the history standards. Here, the interest groups were professors, politicians, educators, and the media. But even granting that the number of "consumers" of this particular product was limited, the professors didn't make an effort to transcend their parochial concerns.

To be fair, many of them didn't make this effort because at the time, they interpreted their audience more narrowly. Akira Iriye, one of the most prominent scholars of international relations in the country, felt that as long as the standards were acceptable to teachers, professional organizations, and above all the community of scholars, then the project could be judged a success. Like many of his colleagues, Iriye distrusted the motives of the politicians who called for national standards. "I didn't think everything should be politicized," he told me. "I had taken for granted that the NEH wasn't under political influence. I had been on NEH committees for twenty years, and there had never been this sort of politicization, so the reaction did come as something of a shock." He nodded to himself as he said this, struck by what he had just said. "It does raise the question of using public funds."

In many ways, the contest was about who owns history. Just as doctors often believe that they own medicine, academics think that they have a proprietary claim to their subject. Professors of the humanities have no trouble acknowledging that many nonacademics are interested in similar subjects. But they don't believe that nonacademics have an equal right to interpret these subjects. It's perfectly fine for a lawyer or a plumber to read a biography of Franklin Roosevelt or a novel by Melville. But if that lawyer or plumber wants to interpret what they've read, then they must defer to the professionals, to the scholarly experts.[31]

For example, when David Denby, a journalist and film critic, wrote a book about his experience reading the great books, he was lambasted by Helen Vendler, a Harvard English professor. Vendler had many quarrels with Denby, but the most significant appeared to be that in her estimation, he didn't know what he was talking about. How could he say anything conclusive about Dante, she wondered, when he couldn't read Italian?[32] While Denby certainly lacked the database, interpretive tools, and linguistic expertise of a professor, he never claimed that his views were "scholarly." But he did implicitly assert the right of a reader to read and react, and that obviously threatened Vendler. He tread on her territory, and she did her best to scare him off. So too do historians try in subtle and not so subtle ways to appropriate history for themselves.

But the standards weren't meant just for historians. The product they produced was deeply at odds with the product other groups expected or wanted. Professors do not exist in a professional culture that encourages them to consider sensibilities other than their own. From graduate school through tenure, academics attend to questions that their colleagues find interesting, using language and methods that their colleagues respect. The professors grappled with standards using the only tools they had, tools they had acquired after years within the guild. For the standards to have been acceptable to other groups, the professors would have had to respect other visions of history. They would have nodded to the notion that history can be morally uplifting. They would have granted that history can provide both inspiring heroes and moral warnings. And they would have spoken to traditional understandings of America even as they added dimensions that have been traditionally absent. Instead, the professors involved with the standards failed to offer nonacademic visions a place at the table.

At best, the standards would have represented multiple agendas. The result would have been akin to a symphony: many instruments, many sounds, one loud, multifaceted product. Leaving the standards to historians, however, was like leaving a symphony to the string section. Even at their best, the strings can never substitute for the other instruments. They do what they do; they play as they are designed to play. Historians think as they are trained to think.

When asked what could have been done differently, both Nash and Crabtree told me that the process was a good one.

Crabtree went so far as to say that if she had to do it again, knowing how the standards would be criticized, she wouldn't have changed the process. I asked Crabtree if she could envision a different way of having drawn up the standards that would have yielded a different result. She answered without hesitation, and without elaboration, "No."

In their book about the controversy, Nash, Crabtree, and Dunn adopt a fatalistic stance. American history, they say, is punctuated by heated debates over interpretation. We are a nation that constantly defines and redefines itself, and wars over history are part of that process. For them, the 1994–1995 standards debate was simply the next installment in an ongoing war, the episode du jour. In spite of the beating the standards took in the media and in Congress, the authors believe that progress was made: "Valuing both critique and commemoration, Americans are liberating themselves from the notion that history is an agreed-upon set of facts and forever a fixed story. . . . One of the jewels in democracy's crown is an educated citizenry that welcomes new harvests of information, unsettling questions, and fresh visions that illuminate our past as well as our present condition."[33]

The professorial establishment that defended the standards rightly dismissed much of Cheney's critique as politically motivated and factually wrong. They saw the uproar as the product not of the standards themselves but of the monomaniacal agenda of conservative ideologues. Nash certainly acknowledged that he and other historians suffered from a lack of media savvy. Cheney and her allies utilized the media and the political process in Washington. That enabled them to trounce the historians in print and in politics. For Nash and his allies, that explained the beating that the standards sustained.

Yet, even here, the historians seem not to have learned any lesson. Clearly, the inability of professors to communicate their vision to the larger society has consequences for how history is understood by the public at large. The lack of media savvy is only one manifestation of the wall separating academics from the society around them, but it is an especially telling one. The media, whether print, radio, or television, is often the only vehicle for the transmission of ideas to the society at large. The disinterest, indeed the scorn, most academics have for expressing themselves via the media shows yet again how the values of the guild trump all other considerations.

Nash ruefully admitted that his capacity to defend the standards was not what it might have been: "I'd never done television debates. I had no experience of this. With few exceptions, none of us have, but our opponents during the standards dispute were very good at it. We don't communicate well. We're used to fifty-minute sound bites because that's the average length of a lecture. When you're in a TV debate, you get fourteen-second sound bites."

Nash then laughed and proceeded to tell me about his first television appearance to answer Cheney's assault: "When I was on the first McNeil-Lehrer debate with Cheney, I was in Sacramento, working with the board of education on curriculum, and I get pulled out of this meeting and someone tells me, 'You're going to be on McNeil-Lehrer an hour from now. There's gonna be a limousine that will take you over to Pacific Satellite relay studio.' So I find myself in front of a purple curtain, and warehouse boxes over here, and a dirty floor over there, and a big camera looking at me. And that's all there is, and I'm miked up, and earplugs. And I can't see Margaret Warner, and I can't see Cheney, because they didn't have a visual relay running back to me. So it's just audio, and I didn't even have a coat and tie. I was up there, I had a casual shirt and a windbreaker.

"The UCLA PR people call me the next morning. 'For Christ's sake, Nash, did you see what Cheney was wearing? She was wearing this snappy red dress and a gold necklace, and her hair was done beautifully. You just looked like shit. Get a power suit. You have to have a blue jacket, and a red tie, and a white shirt. You weren't even looking at the camera. Your eyes were darting this way and that.' So yeah, we don't communicate. I do think that's part of the profession's problem, part of our opportunity. We ought to be more concerned about getting in touch with the public."

I asked Nash if he would think about helping younger colleagues, assistant professors and graduate students, develop these skills. He shook his head. "We all ought to be out there building these bridges, but I can't say that someone without tenure ought to be."

And he's right. If someone without tenure wants tenure, they'd be a fool to devote their energies to working the media, becoming a spokesperson for standards, or debating Lynne Cheney on CNN. They'd be foolish to learn the very skills that might have allowed historians to respond effectively to the accusations made against them in the fall of 1994 and to explain their goals and purposes. Different groups still would have disagreed with them, but at least it would have been a fair fight. But those skills don't count for tenure, and they don't help one advance professionally. They may even be a liability. There's a fine line between being facile on TV and being glib, and glibness is the kiss of death for a scholar.

In numerous ways, the story of the National History Standards Project presents a picture of professors marching to the beat of a very different drummer than other groups in society. And it is a beat only they can hear and appreciate. Public understanding of history is thereby impoverished, and conservative ideologues enjoy an influence disproportionate to their numbers.

Academic insularity has other consequences. The professors who oversaw the standards were the elite of academe. They were superstar scholars, with endowed chairs at the leading research universities. This tier of scholars also controls the professional organizations, and they elaborate policy for the guilds. But as we know, they represent a tiny portion of the professoriate. The average academic is not a professor at Princeton but rather an adjunct at LA Pierce College. These adjuncts and other untenured faculty work under appalling labor conditions, worse even than those of graduate students. The rapid expansion of higher education has produced these conditions, but the same factors that made professors such poor advocates of the standards render them incapable of ameliorating the labor conditions of adjuncts.

If adjuncts were, as the title implies, simply auxiliaries in the academic world, then the issue would not be so signifi-

cant. But a college student today is almost as likely to be educated by adjuncts as by any other type of professor, and
within a few years, adjuncts will account for the majority of
college teaching in the United States. Established professors
lament this development, but they do little to stop it. Academic guilds not only deter professors from communicating
with the larger society; they prevent professors from fixing a
labor problem that threatens to destroy the guilds and im-
perils the most important aspect of higher education today:
classroom teaching.

8

ADJUNCTS AND COMMUNITY COLLEGES

Gloria is finishing her Ph.D. in history in North Dakota. She is thinking about her future. She knows the statistics. She knows that her job options are limited: "I realized when I started this program that the chances were slim of landing a teaching position, but it seems like things are a lot worse than what was presented to me." Still, she knows what she wants: "I have such a burning desire to teach and to make a difference. . . . I have been teaching at the high school level for the past nine years. That isn't the age level for me, and I know I would be more fulfilled as a teacher at the college level."[1]

Gloria is part of a new wave of graduate students who are emerging from Ph.D. programs at state universities with a desire to teach. It's impossible to gauge the number of Glorias in higher education, but there still aren't many. Gloria will discover that, as someone with a Ph.D., she will be in high demand as a teacher. She will find that community colleges in every part of the country will hire her to teach a section of history. If she were an English Ph.D., she'd be hired to teach composition. Gloria added that she has no restrictions as to where she can relocate. Her prospects are bright. For a job as a teacher.

But there's one problem: the salary. If Gloria is lucky, she will be paid $2,000 to teach one section of history. That's only if she's lucky. It's far more likely that she'll earn $1,500. If she can get two sections at one community college and then commute within two hundred miles to another, and if she can teach a total of five sections a term, then perhaps she can earn $15,000 for the year, with no benefits. Because if Gloria is hired, she'll almost certainly be hired as an adjunct.

Adjuncts constitute academia's dirty little secret. Statistics on adjuncts are nearly as difficult to come by as statistics on migrant workers, but just as migrant workers are vital to the economy of agriculture, so too are adjuncts vital to the economy of higher education. The Department of Education estimated that in 1992, 40 percent of all faculty held part-time appointments. Adjuncts account for 64 percent of the faculty at community colleges, and by early next century, that figure is likely to grow to 75 percent. Vermont uses 100 percent adjuncts at their community colleges, while Nevada uses 80 percent. At doctorate-granting institutions, meanwhile, adjuncts do 30 percent of the teaching, though that figure doesn't account for the large numbers of graduate student TAs who teach as well.[2] At minimum, the proportion of adjuncts has doubled since 1970. To repeat, if current trends continue, within a decade the majority of college teaching in the United States will be done by part-time teachers.

The plight of adjuncts has begun to attract some notice in academia. Tenured faculty shake their heads and sigh when the issue is raised at conferences or in discussions. The typical response is "I know, isn't it terrible? We really should do something about that. It's just terrible." But administrators and full-time faculty rarely offer more than empathetic words. That's because without adjuncts, the economy of higher education would collapse.

In the academic food chain, adjuncts are like medieval serfs. As one angry adjunct wrote in the *New York Times* in 1987, "The lords are the official full-time faculty members—the people whose names, degrees, and publications appear in the catalogue. They parade in robes on graduation day and recite the Latin that only William F. Buckley, Jr., can understand. . . . The serfs . . . are the adjunct faculty members, officially part-timers, who in reality often do more teaching than their full-time colleagues. They are the university's lowest paid workers."[3] This is not hyperbole. Adjuncts are paid less than many graduate student TAs are at doctorate-granting universities. A teaching fellow at Harvard earns $3,500 per discussion section, and each graduate student can teach up to six sections each academic year. At Harvard, they also have subsidized health insurance. Adjuncts are certainly paid less than most clerical workers at the school, and they might even earn less than food-service workers, who are normally perceived as being at the bottom of the university employment pool. Many adjuncts have Ph.D.'s, but they make less money than the people who clean the classrooms they teach in.

The reason is simple: Clerical workers, maintenance people, and food-service employees have unions; adjuncts do not. Adjuncts exist as isolated individual laborers. They are part-timers with a vertical relationship with their employer and little contact with each other. They have no support system and no advocates. They work under these conditions because they need the money, no matter how little. They aren't employees, so they can't even collect unemployment when their contracts end.

Several years ago, in a brilliant depiction of unemployed academics, Gary Trudeau's *Doonesbury* showed a college dean standing on a platform with a bullhorn announcing teaching vacancies. Like a plantation foreman looking for day laborers, the dean listed the course and asked for volunteers. One woman raises her hand. The dean shouts at her, "What are your requirements?" She shouts back, "Some respect and a living wage." The dean shouts back, "Anyone else?" "OK, OK," replies the woman, "just some respect."

The reasons for the explosion of adjuncting are transparent. Higher education, particularly in the public sector, exists under continual budgetary pressures. There are several reasons for this, but the primary one is that public higher education is supposed to be accessible to all Americans, regardless of income. That means that the cost of tuition must be kept low. As more Americans attend college, the states are required to provide the space, which means new schools, and that means money for building construction, money for support staff, and money for professors. State budgets, however, are limited by state tax revenue, and higher education is only one of numerous competing needs that state legislatures must meet.

According to a recent study on adjuncting, if a college district wants to offer ten new courses, each of which meets for the standard three hours a week, and if that district hires entry-level full-time faculty to teach those courses, the cost is $38,225. The district can fund the same courses for $16,785 if it hires part-timers at an average of $1,678.45 per course.[4]

Legislatures and education administrators are most likely to be faced with this budgetary choice at the community-college level. That sector of higher education is the fastest growing, and federal initiatives and proposed tax credits will allow even larger numbers of Americans to enroll at community colleges, where the principle of open admissions is firmly entrenched. Low tuition and universal access can exist only if the supply of adjuncts remains steady. If college districts had to hire full-time faculty, state higher education budgets would either need to be supplemented by billions of dollars or tuition would have to rise steeply. Judging from the figures above, schools would have to spend more than twice the money to hire full-time faculty.

Administrators like adjuncts because they are inexpensive, but the proliferation of adjuncting is only possible because universities produce so many Ph.D.'s. Years of oversupply of new Ph.D.'s relative to the number of full-time jobs has created a pool of highly qualified but underemployed labor. If in any given year 20 percent of all job seekers in the humanities land a full-time position, the other 80 percent are left to scramble for one-year replacement positions at best and part-time positions at worst. Most adjunct hiring is done late in the academic season, when those without jobs have become fairly desperate.

Getting hired as an adjunct is uncomplicated and often random. An unemployed Ph.D., or underfunded graduate student, sends a curriculum vitae and references to the department chair or the human resources office of local colleges and universities. If the application is for the fall term, then sometime between May and August, when the department chair has a sense of fall enrollments, he or she goes through the pile of c.v.'s and selects those from applicants who seem able to teach. A candidate will probably be called for an interview and then offered a job. That's about the extent of the evaluation. Though each full-time job, even at a community college, attracts anywhere from a hundred to five hundred applicants, part-time jobs are plentiful and relatively easy to obtain. The quality of adjunct teaching varies widely. Some adjuncts may have been teaching for years, or they may have been hired without any previous teaching experience whatsoever. Faced with ten slots to fill, department chairs take what they can get, and they usually look at c.v.'s for minimum qualifications. Although adjuncts are hired to teach, very few places screen applicants to ensure that they can teach.

That's because few places have the resources or the time to do this screening. If a school is trying to save money by using adjuncts, it's unlikely to spend money trying to hire the best adjuncts. Furthermore, given the supply-demand ratio at the adjunct level, the school doesn't have the flexibility to search for the best. The only latitude a department chair has is to eliminate the absolutely unqualified and the totally unfit.

As a graduate student at Harvard, I applied to teach a summer course at the University of Massachusetts at Boston. An immense, hulking mass of red brick and cinder block that juts into Boston's bay, UMass-Boston is a commuter school, vintage 1965. I sent in my vitae, waited a month, and got a call from the chair of the department. An amiable, decent man, he had received his Ph.D. in the 1960s at the University of Wisconsin at Madison and had taught at Boston ever since. We chatted about mutual acquaintances, and after half an hour, he offered me a course.

For the next three years, I taught a course on U.S. foreign relations each summer. One fall, I also taught the introductory Western history survey. The summer-school courses went fairly well—most of the students were full-time college kids getting extra credits between terms—but the Western civilization course was a disaster. Twenty students began the course, but only thirteen finished. The school was being renovated during the term, and we had to move to a different classroom every few weeks. Most of the time, the building was filled with paint fumes.

The real problem, however, was me. I designed the course around big ideas. With one three-hour class every Tuesday night and three thousand years of history to cover, it was impossible to cover anything in great depth. The syllabus went something like this: "Week 1: Origins; Week 2: The Greeks; Week 3: The Romans." Rather than insist on detail, I tried to paint with broad brushstrokes. And rather than using a textbook, I assigned several smaller books, each focused on a particular topic, along with some documents from the period. Half the students loved the material; the other half had no idea what was going on. I assumed going in that the students would know how to read a book and distinguish between important events and facts and less vital details, names, and places. That assumption was a mistake.

Students at elite schools are not necessarily smarter than students at less selective schools, but they do have several advantages. Not only are they more affluent, they also have had better secondary educations, and they arrive at places like Stanford and Georgetown secure in their ability to learn new material. They think they're smart, and they're not afraid to speak about things that they don't know much about. They're also extremely grade conscious and ambitious. But students who take a night course at a local college are less likely to be convinced of their brilliance. On the contrary, they often lack self-confidence in their abilities, and this makes it hard for them to work their way through difficult ideas and concepts. Not because they can't, but rather because they don't believe they can.

Not only was the course too advanced for many of the students, but several of them didn't speak English that well. After three classes, one student stopped coming. So I called his home and after several tries finally reached him. After a monosyllabic conversation, I realized that he literally didn't understand me, and I learned from the school registrar that he had recently immigrated from Taiwan. I could not have done much about the students who didn't know English. Judging from the voluminous postings on Internet newsgroups recounting teaching horror stories, it's clear that English comprehension is a problem at college just as it is in secondary schools. In fact, English comprehension is sometimes a problem with the teachers themselves, and students frequently complain that they can't understand their professors. The United States now draws hundreds of thousands of undergraduates and graduate students from around the world, and not all of them speak fluent English.

Nonetheless, I could have done a much better job designing the course and presenting the material if I had known what to expect. I was fortunate that the summer-school students were for the most part capable. Perhaps that was because of the different demographics of summer school, and perhaps it was because I was teaching an upper-level course open only to advanced history majors. The night-school extension course drew a different type of student, and I was unprepared and ill equipped for the job.

Still, I was hired, and if I had taught the course again, I would have integrated the lessons from the first go-round and tried to rectify the problems. But it would have been up to me, and if I had thought that the first time was just fine, I could have offered the exact same course with the same books and the same approach, and no one at UMass-Boston would have been the wiser. No one checked my syllabus or visited a class. I wasn't asked to give out evaluation forms, and no student complained. Having been hired once, I would have been rehired if enrollments demanded it. Unless I had done something criminal or outrageous, I could have kept that job, paying $2,500 per course, indefinitely.

During those summers and that fall, I never met another adjunct. I saw their names on departmental lists of courses offered, but I never saw them, heard about them, or talked with them. That isolation may have been extreme, but it was hardly unusual for adjunct teaching. And the lack of over-sight is typical.

In its current form, adjuncting hurts students and the ad-juncts themselves. Because there is so little oversight, it is nearly impossible for a student to predict whether a class taught by an adjunct will be worth the time and money. Stu-dents paying $500 for a night-school course at a local college have no way of knowing whether they are purchasing a Mer-cedes or a lemon. By the time they figure out that the adjunct professor is incompetent, the best they can hope for is to get some of their money back when they withdraw from the course. It will be too late to sign up for another course until the following term.

The nature of adjuncting means that a significant number of college students in the United States have less than com-petent teachers. Those adjuncts who are capable may not be available to their students, especially if they are commuting to several different schools many miles apart. And capable or not, adjuncts have little reason to be loyal to the institution that pays them. They are given no benefits, no respect, no of-fice, and little money. They rarely interact with other faculty, and when they do, they are treated much like temp workers at a corporate office.

At the same time, thousands of adjuncts are wonderful teachers. They set aside generous amounts of time for meet-ings with students; they plan their classes meticulously, go over writing assignments with great care, offer to read drafts of papers and provide detailed feedback, and they care. At every level of higher education, students say that the best teachers are the ones who are passionate about the subject and who respect their students. Many of these teachers are part-time adjuncts barely eking out a living, and many are happily teaching full-time in community colleges.

Thousands of graduate students and adjuncts discover their calling in the classroom. "I'm a Ph.D. candidate in English," writes Wendy, "and am finishing my first year teaching at East Los Angeles College. It has been an incredible experience, which has satisfied all of my needs as a teacher and a scholar. After all those years of grad school, which seemed to focus more on developing my c.v. than my mind (or spirit), I had serious doubts about remaining in academia. Where was the collegiality, the intellectual stimulation that I thought (silly me) would be an inherent part of academic life? Where was the sense that my work and my teaching actually made a difference in the world? Certainly not in my experiences at conferences. [Then] I was hired at East LA. When people ask me how I like teaching at a two-year, my stock answer has become: 'If I had known this was waiting for me, I would never have crabbed for a minute about grad school.' My students are 80 percent Latino. They differ from the students I taught at several universities, and they are unbelievably involved and eager to learn."[5]

Even if some graduate students love adjuncting and love teaching at a community college, they may not love it after five years. The teaching responsibilities are heavy, and the students demanding, and once again, the pay barely suffices for survival. And teaching as an adjunct, or even teaching full-time at a community college, may damage your future job prospects at other levels in the academic system. Stories abound of graduate students being advised by their doctoral advisors not to take a job at a community college if they want to be seriously considered as a candidate for a job at a four-year college. For recent Ph.D.'s, the number of hours they spend in the classroom as adjuncts precludes any substantial research projects. But search committees at four-year schools look at research first when evaluating applicants.

In addition to creating a time crunch that forces research and writing onto a back burner, part-time teaching isn't glamorous. It doesn't make a candidate more attractive. People who have been on the job market for several years without landing a full-time job start to be seen as damaged goods, and their status as adjuncts becomes a mark against them. They may be superlative lecturers and caring educators, but the fact that they work as part-timers can make them less appealing in the eyes of the profession.

The sensitivity of academics to hierarchy manifests itself in many ways, but if you want to observe one of the most unpleasant demonstrations of academic snobbery, go to a major academic conference and watch how people react to one another. Let's say a panel delivers three papers to an audience of seventy-five. At the end of the formal presentation, the audience will ask questions. People stand and identify themselves. Those who have "respectable" qualifications will elicit nods of agreement or sighs of disagreement, and others might approach them afterwards to continue the conversation. But if you stand up and say that you are from No-Name Community College, and even worse, if you say you are an adjunct, eyes glaze over. The sensation is palpable and familiar to anyone who's attended these events.[6]

Though the growth of higher education may be in the community college or lower-level state systems, the assumptions of academia remain the same as they've been for decades. Consciously or not, most academics presume that the best and the brightest get hired by the best schools. The talented teach at Ivy League schools or exclusive liberal arts colleges; the next level end up at schools like those in the Big Ten. Below these are regional schools like Western Michigan, and then mediocre institutions like Brooklyn Community College or East Los Angeles. Great minds find a home at the great schools. Nice, decent teachers land jobs at regional schools, and those who really ought to be in another profession muddle though as adjuncts.

Though unattractive, these prejudices are deeply entrenched, even though the reality of academic employment means that they have little basis in fact. It is true that the elite schools hire the most talented. But there are far more of the most talented than there are jobs, and those who don't get one do what they can to make a living. Over time, most of those who end up at elite schools come to view themselves as there because of their talent and not because of luck or being at the right place at the right time. When they see a recent Ph.D. from a reputable university making the rounds at conferences, trying to get hired part-time, they recoil. If they were honest with themselves, they might say, "There but for the grace of God go I."

The patterns of academic employment aren't completely random, and many adjuncts probably aren't suitable for the best jobs. That doesn't excuse the biases against them or the lack of attention that academic guilds pay to adjunct labor conditions. The guilds spend considerable time countering the slightest erosions of tenure, but they rarely act as advocates for part-timers. The guild approach to employment conditions can be described as "tenure or bust." The American Association of University Professors has issued a statement on part-time labor in which it deplores the dependence on adjuncts and calls for improved pay, basic benefits, and more security. Yet part-time employment clearly isn't a priority for the AAUP or any other professional organization. The major professional journals barely register the existence of community colleges, let alone adjuncts, and the same professors who write the AAUP's mission statements turn around and hire ten adjuncts to fill lower-level lecture courses at their understaffed universities.[7]

The distrust for any emendations of the tenure system makes it difficult if not impossible for professors and academic organizations to champion the cause of part-time labor. In Texas and Minnesota, the faculty believed that the plans to alter tenure originated with anti-intellectual conservatives bent on destroying academic freedom. Professors at these places gave no credence to the notion that there were real financial problems. They did not concede that university trustees confronted a conundrum of rising enrollments and stagnant budgets and that proposals to loosen tenure arose from genuine need for financial flexibility. Instead, professors interpreted the attempt to revise tenure as an assault on their way of life and freedom of speech.

"Should the administration have the ability to act selectively to reduce a faculty member's salary, without needing to establish cause under safeguards of academic due process," stated the AAUP in response to proposals at the University of Minnesota, "a significant underpinning for principles of academic freedom and tenure at that institution would be lacking."[8] Tenured full-time professors tend to think of academic employment in absolute terms. For them, it is all or nothing. Devoting their resources and time to improving the labor conditions of adjuncts would mean accepting that for many schools, supporting tenured research scholars is not economically viable.

The very faculty denouncing the trustees in Minnesota are perfectly capable of hiring and firing adjuncts by the hundreds. They'd like to have the money to hire more full-time faculty, but they don't like the cost of having that money. The only source of that money is their salaries. That money, however, is untouchable, because of academic freedom. Not surprisingly, these professors are not about to man the barricades for adjuncts. No. Doing that would be self-defeating. Without adjuncts, either these tenured faculty would have to teach more or they would have to give up some of the benefits that come with tenure.

But state legislatures aren't about to reform adjuncting either, and neither are regents, trustees, or college presidents. They can't promise open access and affordable tuition and at the same time pay for full-time faculty where adjuncts now are. The City University of New York, which for the past twenty years has tried to honor the principle of enrollment to all, relies on more than six thousand adjuncts.[9] As long as graduate students and unemployed Ph.D.'s keep applying for part-time jobs, and as long as department chairs and administrators can put them in classrooms for less than $2,000 a course, then adjuncting will continue. Just as everyone laments the sorry state of migrant workers—the erratic work, the poor pay, the chattel-like treatment—academics decry the status of adjuncts and then blithely take advantage of them.

What message does that send to students and to professors? That teaching is not worth as much as cooking at a state university? That college professors deserve only a third of the wages and none of the security that high school and grade school teachers have? That it's regrettable but not that regrettable that 75 percent of community college teachers live at or below the poverty level?

Unions represent one possible avenue of change, but organizing adjuncts nationally would strain the capacities of the most gifted organizers. Adjuncts are transient. They often have multiple employers for short periods of time. They teach in different subjects, each with different requirements and different professional organizations that compete with one another more than they work together. Unions also have a tendency to become corporate and bureaucratic. Universities are already stultifyingly bureaucratic, and adding another layer may not be wise.

Most of all, unions may be unnecessary because academic guilds already possess an infrastructure of collective bargaining. Universities employ the best lobbyists money can buy when appropriations bills are debated in state assemblies or in Congress. Professional organizations such as the AAUP are also skilled at advocacy at the national and local levels. Mechanisms do exist to put pressure on administrators and legislatures to institute minimum labor guidelines for adjuncts. It's just that no one utilizes these to improve the situation of adjuncts.

The use of part-timers maintains the equilibrium of the academic economy, but the cost is rising. Community colleges depend on adjuncts, yet only community colleges unequivocally embrace teaching as their sole mission. The lip service given to adjunct labor conditions implicitly says that teaching is not a priority for academic guilds. The president of the AHA and the MLA or a spokesperson for the AAUP would object heartily to that statement. But commitment to teaching requires a commitment to adjuncts, and other than kind words, these organizations offer nothing to part-timers. Actions do indeed speak louder than words, and the actions of these organizations speak volumes.

The professional organizations and the elite of academia neglect the situation of adjuncting, but they no longer represent the sentiments of most professors. According to an extensive survey of nearly thirty-four thousand professors (a quarter of whom teach humanities) at over 380 institutions, being a good teacher is far and away the most important professional goal. Ninety-nine percent of those surveyed said that they feel it is essential to be a good teacher. Eighty-seven percent said that it was essential to be a good colleague. But only 55 percent said that it was essential to be a good researcher, and 42 percent said this of providing services to the community. While 54 percent said that tenure is necessary to attract the best minds to academe, 38 percent agreed that tenure "is an outmoded concept." As for their goals, 61 percent felt it essential to "prepare students for responsible citizenship."[10]

These findings are astonishing in light of the priorities of the guilds. They undercut the definition of the professor that academic elites and professional organizations champion and defend. The center may be holding, but rumblings can be heard on the periphery. Change is coming at the academic equivalent of the grass-roots level. Only recently have the guilds begun to notice what's going on at the large state universities and the community colleges, and what they see is a world that bears little resemblance to the quadrangles the research scholar occupies. Without grass-roots activity, there can be no change, but unless the guilds begin to shift their energies to place adjuncts, community colleges, and teaching at the center of professional life, community colleges will be staffed by part-timers.

During the 1990s, the president of the United States, the National Governors Conference, Republicans and Democrats in the United States Congress, and numerous business leaders added standards and universal college education to the national political agenda. These powerful groups in society have enunciated a vision for college education. They believe that at least two years of college are vital to the health of the United States; they think that universal college education will strengthen the bonds of citizenship and enhance the skills of American workers, thereby benefiting the country socially and economically.

We've seen that academic guilds do not share this vision of higher education. They may not disagree that college can provide these benefits, but they do not define academia primarily in terms of the service it can do for the larger society. The one exception within academia is the community college system. Imagine. The layer of academia held in the lowest regard by the guilds is the layer most valued by society at large.

Adding to the irony, community colleges are far more likely to embrace the notion of public service than are other schools. Community colleges have a long tradition of serving as "people's colleges." They were and continue to be a manifestation of American democracy expressed through education. In this sense, community colleges act as a leveling device. Regardless of class, race, or even of prior academic performance, any American citizen and any immigrant living in the United States can attend college and earn a degree. Community colleges exist for the sole purpose of helping people get an education, and faculty are hired for the sole purpose of teaching whoever takes a seat in the classroom.[11] Of course we shouldn't idolize the community college (though judging from attitudes in the guilds and in the press, there's no immediate danger of that). Some of the more bizarre and ridiculous education-school philosophies about teaching find a welcome home at community colleges. The process-content debate was an issue during the development of the national history standards, but it's an even larger problem at places like East Los Angeles or Bunker Hill College. Because of the transitory nature of the community college faculty, administrators determine the reigning philosophies, and they often import management techniques acquired from business and apply them to the classroom with wildly uneven results.

Community colleges are expected either to provide vocational training or to prepare students for a four-year university, and state education officials assess the performance of these colleges either by job-placement statistics or by acceptance rates at four-year schools. In order for these statistics to shine, students have to graduate, and graduate with good grades. Given the disparate quality of the students who enroll, the pressure for high graduation rates often means that poor students are given good grades. Though the mission of the community college is education, institutional imperatives sometimes make that mission impossible.

Still, nearly half of all undergraduates pass through community colleges, and education is the priority. There may be some confusion about what constitutes an education, but community colleges are not the source of that confusion. American education from nursery school through graduate school suffers from ambivalence. People entrust schools with their most extraordinary hopes for their children, for themselves, and for the country's future. They look to school as the vehicle for social mobility, and they believe that school provides the tools for success in society.

This points to a final issue that has hovered in the background so far. We've talked about students, their belief that college equals a job, and their amorphous expectations of the humanities. We've delved into the academic guilds and looked at how removed professors are from society. There's a final component: society itself. In a country of more than 250 million people, it's impossible to talk of one society, thinking and acting in one way. But we can discern general attitudes. These attitudes, and how we perceive them, shape our behavior, and they shape higher education in this country.

9
SOCIETY AND HIGHER EDUCATION

In his state of the union speech in January 1997, President William Jefferson Clinton outlined his goals for his second term: Education would be the number one priority of his administration. Being the education president has become something of a habit for recent occupants of the Oval Office. There's nothing controversial about a president committing himself to education, and no political leader takes a stand against education.

Clinton went further than his predecessors, however. He pledged "to make the thirteenth and fourteenth years of education—at least two years of college—just as universal in America by the twenty-first century as a high school education is today." He called for millions of dollars in "Hope Scholarships," tax credits of $1,500 a year for two years to help middle-income families pay for college. After some raised eyebrows among the Republican leadership in Congress, these Hope Scholarships were funded in the bipartisan budget agreement of 1997.[1] In his state of the union address a year later in 1998, Clinton again spoke of college as an American birthright.

Some of the reasons for this initiative have been discussed. All indicators demonstrate that college graduates earn significantly more than those without a college degree. Many employers won't even consider hiring someone without a B.A., let alone an associate's degree. In a country attached to notions of advancement based on merit, people perceive education as the path to success. These impressions of a college degree may be self-fulfilling. If you can't get a good job without college, then college must be what gets you a good job. If the most successful people have graduated from college, then college must be the avenue to success.[2]

The ability of America to compete internationally also looms large in the push toward universal higher education. Few countries send as high a proportion of its citizens to college. In many parts of the world, higher education belongs to a select elite, with admission determined either by social class or by national exams, administered to all secondary school students in their late teens. In France, for example, students completing their secondary schooling take a standardized baccalaureate exam. Those who perform well get admitted to the best universities; those in the next percentile gain admission to polytechnics and equivalent schools; and those who perform below a certain score are refused admission, though they can retake the exam in subsequent years. Similar national screening mechanisms exist in other countries.

Americans, however, are ambivalent and suspicious about such standards and screening mechanisms, even voluntary ones. The tradition of local control over education is strong in the United States. Parents and community leaders have always resisted a nationally mandated curriculum, and that is one reason why the most popular educational philosophies have stressed process rather than content.[3] Local communities don't want to be told what their students must learn, and they tend to gravitate toward educational strategies that emphasize the limitless possibilities of each individual. For this reason, perhaps, education in this country has been framed by thinkers such as John Dewey rather than by tests such as the baccalaureate. Dewey's pragmatism left wide room for local variance, while standardized tests offer none.[4]

The SAT is a major exception to this generalization. To gain admission to an elite school, high SAT scores are imperative. And the SAT is standardized nationally. But unlike such tests in other countries, poor performance on the SAT does not close the door to higher education; it simply prevents a student from going to places like Harvard, Yale, or Berkeley.

Washington's sponsorship of higher education stems from the belief that economic competitiveness and college education are somehow connected. Yet to be competitive, you have to meet minimum standards, whether the market is domestic or international. Politicians and business leaders are concerned about the "cognitive ability" of workers, about their ability to learn, think, and then act. These skills don't just accrue naturally because a person obtains a two-letter suffix following their name. John Smith, B.A., isn't necessarily any more capable than John Smith. It isn't the degree that provides some sort of magical advantage. It's the skills that a person who receives the degree ought to have acquired.

This leads to a paradox. As envisioned by the president, by the governors, by the Congress, by parents, by business leaders, and by Americans in general, a college education ought to be available to all Americans, regardless of class, income, and yes, ability. As a result, millions of students will get degrees, and learn some basic history, science, and math, and so be better able to perform the jobs demanded by the information age. But the way that higher education is being used by society also guarantees that the problems that beset education at all levels in the United States will simply be pushed one notch further up.

Professors teaching their first class in English composition or introductory history at most colleges in the United States usually come away from the experience dismayed and astonished. "They can't write!" "They can't read!" "They can't think!" These problems might be expected of students whose first language isn't English, whose cognitive abilities are fine but whose capacity to express these in a foreign tongue are hampered by limited vocabulary and poor syntax. What truly surprises most first-time professors is the number of English-speaking college students who don't know how to think, read, or write.

These students are all high school graduates. Presumably, all of them took English and writing courses; all of them took some history or civics, some math, some science. These subjects are mandated by most local boards of education. Though there are no reliable statistics, it may be that more than half of all incoming college students at the community college and lower-tier state level don't possess basic English and cognitive skills.

The literature on the crisis of American schools is vast. While some suburban schools succeed brilliantly, public schools in urban and rural areas have not been able to achieve basic goals of student competency. Within the literature, there are substantial disagreements about who or what is responsible for the state of our schools. Fingers are pointed at incompetent teachers, lazy kids, crumbling buildings, corrupt school boards, powerful custodial unions, misguided superintendents, and morally weak parents. Everyone agrees that there is a problem, but consensus about why has proved elusive.

Whatever the causes, people have begun to look to higher education as the solution. Debates over higher education and debates on school education are segregated in the United States. Specialists on one rarely talk with specialists on the other; other than the few who write textbooks, professors have minimal contact with schoolteachers; and education bureaucracies erect a wall between higher education and secondary education departments as high as the one separating the army from the navy in the Pentagon.

In the face of less than stellar results in primary and secondary education, Americans seem to be saying, "How about two more years of school?" What the high schools fail to teach, community colleges and public universities will provide. Eighteen-year-olds can't write an essay after marching down the aisle? Send them to Comp 101. High-schoolers can't read a chapter of a book and make sense of the argument? Send them to Intro to American History, or English Lit A.

Community colleges may embrace an ethos of public service, but that does not mean that they are equipped to perform the function of remedial education. The City University of New York spent the past decades trying to balance high standards with the deficient preparation of its incoming freshmen. It spent millions of dollars to hire faculty and recalibrate the curriculum in order to teach students basic literacy and composition. As the difficulties mounted, the political support for remedial education at CUNY has eroded.[5] Newer state schools and community colleges have an easier time. Their curriculum and course offerings are geared from the outset to remedial education.

The faculty, however, lack the teacher training necessary for basic skills education. An upper-level history or English course assumes that the students enrolled have some prior knowledge of the subject matter and the skills to do the required reading, writing, and exams. Graduate students and professors view their task as conveying information to students who are capable of integrating it. They analyze that information and ask the students to think about different interpretations. Some professors sparkle when they lecture; others put their students to sleep. But with few exceptions, they do know their subject.

Emerging from graduate school, however, they don't know how to teach writing; they don't know how to teach reading; and they have only a vague sense of how to teach thinking. At most, they usually can teach their students how to analyze material the way specialists in the particular subject analyze it. Historians can show students how to evaluate a historical document; literature professors provide students with a road map for reading a novel.

Teaching basic skills like composition and reading, especially if the students aren't native English speakers, requires training. Students need to learn specific techniques. While a historian who's an expert on the Civil War might be able to show his students how to read, left to his own devices, he will be just as likely to confuse as to illuminate. A writing specialist uses methods that have been derived from years of hit-and-miss experiments, and her success rate will be higher than someone who improvises. In order for these extra years of school to fulfill society's expectations, students have to emerge from those two years with the skills they didn't obtain in high school. The adjuncts and professors who are delegated to teach them, however, are less qualified than high school teachers to impart those skills.

Higher education seems like the perfect answer to an intractable problem. Decades of drastic changes and incremental reforms haven't noticeably improved the achievement level of high schools, but public higher education still hasn't lost is shine. The public still retains romantic notions of college and still sees a college degree as a special achievement. Americans feel good about their universities, and higher education is rightly seen as one of the more productive sectors of society.[6]

In an era where distrust of government is at an all-time high,[7] a majority of people support government funding of higher education.[8] Twenty-seven percent of the general public has "a great deal of confidence" in the people running colleges and universities; and another 50 percent have some confidence. Only the military, the Supreme Court, and the medical profession rank higher.[9] Middle-class parents take great pride in seeing their children in college, and immigrants send their children to college as a symbol of integration into American society. While there are controversies at specific schools or over particular events, higher education is held in greater esteem than most major institutions or most sectors of society.

Given these attitudes, it's not surprising that everyone from the president to the proverbial man on the street supports more college for more people. Disenchanted with public high schools, people invest their hopes and dreams in institutions they still trust and respect. People believe in college with an optimism that has all but vanished in other areas of life. They believe in the American dream fulfilled by education. They are willing to pay substantial sums of money for these dreams, and in return colleges are saying, yes, we will educate you, and give you time to think, learn, and grow, give you the skills you need, and award you the ticket to your future.

People look to college not just for skills but for more amorphous things they believe they lack. Society turns to higher education not just to compensate for high schools but to unite people who otherwise seem so at odds with one another. Listening to the rhetoric that surrounds higher education, one would think that college is family, church, village, and nation all rolled into one. Somehow, by placing everyone who is eighteen years old in college, and then immigrants and mature students, we will become one nation with one vision. College is treated as the last and best hope for turning atomized individuals with limited abilities into Americans with boundless ambitions.

Under this rubric, the classroom acts as training wheels for citizenship. If the university represents the last chance to forge a nation, then of course the minutiae of the curriculum and the worldview of professors will be issues of national security. Of course conservatives will shout that professors who try to expose the seamier sides of our culture are actually destroying what little unity we have.[10] Of course leftist professors will denounce "traditional" narratives as part of a power structure that keeps the business class rich and wages for the rest stagnant, and of course they will try to use the classroom to redress the imbalances they see in the society at large.[11]

These perspectives raise the stakes of higher education, and they explain the intensity of the culture war over what is to be taught and how. Both radical and conservative ideologues invest college with the power to define society. The ideas that men and women learn in the classroom will form the template for the way they act in society. If one believes this, then the humanities are what truly matters in higher education, because how one understands history and culture determines how one understands the workings of society. Admiration for heroes and for the achievements of states leads ineluctably to a belief in the individual and deference to the state. History "from the ground up," one that shows the sufferings of the disenfranchised and their efforts to carve out lives of self-respect against the vehement resistance of elites, leads naturally to a resistance against the state and a disinclination to support it.[12]

The classroom is important, but there is little evidence that it exercises such a dramatic influence on students' lives. A soft-spoken, shy young man may come home after his first term at Berkeley preaching Marx at the dinner table and denouncing his parents for their bourgeois values, but four years later, he'll probably go shopping with his parents for his first interview suit. His freshman Marxism may owe something to reading Marx in one of his classes, but it also owes something to his roommates and his friends, many of whom might be science majors who picked up Marx at a café on Telegraph Avenue. The same story could be told in Cambridge, Ann Arbor, Austin, Boulder, or Madison.

Colleges themselves foster these images. Promotional literature sent out to high school seniors paints college as a transformative experience. Students are promised independence, enlightenment, and success. From the newest community college to Harvard, college brochures contain pictures of students frolicking in the sun next to gleaming buildings, students walking in pairs books in tow, and students sitting in class with thoughtful expressions on their faces. Higher education sells itself as a world of limitless possibilities; it offers students an opportunity to step outside of society in order to reenter it enhanced, better, more able.[13]

Students and parents have an almost mystical belief in the power of college. Students routinely talk of "finding themselves" and "knowing themselves." I've heard eighteen-year-olds and forty-year-olds say that at college they hope to discover who they are, that they see college as an opportunity to find their calling in life. Mature students attending college after years in the workforce often spend a year or two trying to locate that intangible something they thought college provided, some sense of self-worth, some grounding. They look at their younger peers and wonder if they are missing something, a certain attitude, a look in the eye, imperceptible body language, something that will give them the edge in life they feel they've lacked.

Of course, many students attend college without a second thought and go about the experience without much introspection or romance. Many mature students have specific goals. They plan to get a degree so that they can apply for that management job at the company they've worked at for years. Still, even the utilitarian students, the ones who don't buy into the images or much care about those pictures in the glossy brochures, even these see college as a process that will change them for the better.

Professors do their part to foster these impressions. According to the president and secretary of the AAUP in their recommendations to Congress in 1996, "Students who have been educated in American universities and colleges should be well prepared to encounter the world's complexities and to contribute something of worth in their chosen fields. Postsecondary education should continue not only to convey information, but also to inspire curiosity, to encourage critical thinking, and to elicit the most important questions—the ones that, as of yet, have no answers."[14]

Colleges and universities throughout the country have begun to emphasize ethics, morality, and community responsibility. The provost of the University of Southern California, Lloyd Armstrong, says of the school's mission, "All of us are having to think very hard about how you can help people live together. That's just about the highest priority there is." Bobbi Patterson, an assistant professor of religion at Emory, in Atlanta, believes that the university has an obligation to be moral: "We must decide that a common moral landscape at Emory is a priority," she wrote, "and decide that the intellectual life requires moral development." And University of Pennsylvania president Judith Rodin is trying to return to Benjamin Franklin's ideal of service as an integral component of teaching and learning.[15]

The notion that universities have a responsibility to produce moral graduates is hardly new. If anything, that was the dominant mission of the American university in previous centuries. Colleges were part of the colonial religious establishments, and they had an explicitly religious purpose. While that faded by the early twentieth century, it never really disappeared, and the contemporary emphasis on moral uplift is part of the rising tide of religion in society as a whole.[16]

These various threads combine to form a richly textured tapestry, but attractive though it is, it's also susceptible to fraying. Like dressing up a little boy for a special event, colleges can package their students to make them look and feel educated, moral, and prepared for what life has to offer. Students want to believe that college is the answer to life's uncertainties; parents hope that the money they spend will guarantee their sons and daughters a stable future; and our elected representatives look to education as a cure for multiple social ills.

College can be a wonderful experience. It can open doors to realms that students have indeed only dreamed of. It can provide access to information and skills that, put to good use, enable students to pursue their ambitions. The classroom can be a forum for serious thought about history, culture, morality, religion, science, and the future. In two or four years of college, students often do grow wiser, and they learn about themselves and the world around them.

That said, the goals we have for higher education are unrealistic, and many of our images have only a tenuous relationship to reality. The humanities are important, but not nearly as important as some people believe. It's nice to believe that a common curriculum produces a common identity, but there's never been either in the United States.[17] Reading Plato is a wonderful experience, one that everyone should have if they have the time and inclination. But if most people don't read Plato, society as we know it won't collapse, and people will somehow stumble through life, occasionally making mistakes and very often contributing meaningfully to society and their communities.

As for moral uplift, professors can certainly prod students to contemplate difficult moral and ethical issues. They can also, by example, show students that it is possible to have strong disagreements with other people and still sit next to them. Perhaps the most important lesson that humanities classes offer is that in a democracy that values free expression, disagreement is natural and healthy. Professors and administrators who preach moral uplift, however, are likely to find students unreceptive. As Bill Brands's students at Texas A&M reminded me, they have their own minds, and they want to decide for themselves what they think is right and wrong. Attempts to inculcate an explicit moral code usually fail.

At a more pragmatic level, does college truly lead to better jobs? Not necessarily. The more people go to college, the less a college degree is worth. Though college graduates definitely earn more than high school graduates, more and more businesses require a college degree for jobs that used to be performed by people without degrees. It's not unheard of for bookstores to insist on some college experience for their applicants, and many positions, regardless of the nature of the business, are open only to college graduates. Yet the salary of these jobs is often minimal, and the types of jobs that count as "college jobs" would surprise many people.

The Bureau of Labor Statistics defines the following as college jobs: manager of a Blockbuster video store, legal secretary, insurance claims adjuster. Not all college graduates get "college jobs." Some end up waiting tables, or selling clothing, or driving vans—jobs that are perfectly feasible ways of making a living but that don't seem to require a college education and the attendant tens of thousands of dollars' worth of debt. Each year, college graduates enter the workforce and find themselves working at jobs very different from the ones they thought college was preparing them for.[18] Given a choice between hiring a college graduate and a high school graduate, most businesses will chose the former, regardless of the job. Why not? If you can get someone better qualified for the same money, that's what you do. You never know when that asset will be needed.

As higher education has evolved, Americans have periodically debated the question of vocational education. For the most part, explicitly vocational education offends Americans. It seems to close avenues rather than open them, and to a degree it does. Yet millions of students at community colleges and state schools slot themselves into a de facto vocational track. They take courses and degrees that prepare them to be accountants, physical therapists, computer programmers, system managers, and hundreds of other occupations. Many of these require very specialized skills and years of training. Without suffering from the uncomfortable connotations of the label "vocational," these students willingly and purposefully eschew a liberal arts education. The sheer number of students who pursue degrees that equip them for specific jobs indicates that various forms of vocational education are now a reality.

Many of these students still want the "college experience," with dorms, football teams, fraternities, and all the other accoutrements. But others do not want these things; they want skills for jobs. Period. The information age demands an ever more capable workforce, but many of the skills required aren't taught in the classroom. While having a high proportion of the populace attend college might be beneficial in terms of innovations and job flexibility, it is still unclear why everyone ought to go to college. Some have been fairly blunt in their skepticism, like former president of Boston University John Silber, who said that many Americans are too "stupid" to go to college. "What about people who want to be lab technicians or plumbers?" Silber asked in response to Clinton's proposals.[19] Silber's views are extreme and his tact is nonexistent, but he poses a legitimate question. Is universal higher education necessary?

We need to have a serious discussion about this issue, and we are not having it. Such a discussion would evaluate all aspects of higher education, including vocational training and the role of the liberal arts. For the moment, we are plunging into the universities without scrutinizing the benefits and the costs. Rhetoric about jobs and skills propels the political establishment, and amorphous beliefs in what college offers draw students. As we contemplate devoting an increasing chunk of our national resources to higher education, we ought to stop for a moment. We need to think about what we expect from higher education and look hard and long at what higher education actually does.

Universities are vibrant institutions. They house creative minds and bodies, and they are a source of strength and imagination. They generate medical and scientific innovations; they offer a home to novelists and poets; they produce athletes and scholars, entrepreneurs and managers. They are rarely, however, a panacea for spiritual ennui and lack of direction. They seldom implant a sense of self where none exists. They cannot build or destroy communities, and they can provide little comfort during those dark nights of the soul. Higher education is a resource. Like any resource, it can be used appropriately or not. At best, colleges provide a setting for thought and analysis, and they bring people together who might not otherwise interact. They create a public sphere for people to learn and discover.

Sending every single American to college, however, will no more ensure productive, happy citizens than sending them to good grade schools or good high schools will. No institution has the capacity to grant people self-knowledge or confidence, and placing these demands on higher education is a sure recipe for mass disillusionment decades from now.

CONCLUSION

So whose college is it anyway? Who owns the university? Who will determine what college is for? Trustees? College presidents? Students? Graduate students? Parents? Politicians? Taxpayers? State legislatures? Professors?

The answer is: all of the above.

All of these groups have a vested interest in higher education. All of them care, and with good reason, about what is taught and how it is taught. All of them look at college as a vital force in society, and all of them believe that our identity and success as a nation are somehow tied to what goes on in the college classroom.

Some of our expectations of higher education are inflated, but the belief that college constitutes one pillar of our identity isn't. Contrary to what certain conservatives claim, the United States has always been characterized by ethnic, racial, and linguistic diversity. But contrary to what some liberals assert, primary and secondary schools have been a common ground, uniting us in a shared experience, though never a shared curriculum. Now higher education must be added to the list of shared experiences. We are approaching a point where higher education is as universal as grade school. The preponderance of the growth lies in the public sector, yet most of our images and expectations of college derive from the small, private, elite liberal arts college.

Culturally, we have not yet caught up to the democratization of higher education. Arguments about the curriculum, about standards, about what should be taught and how are still framed by ivy, while most of the 3,500 institutions of higher learning are not. Though the students who attend the elite schools will go on to exert an influence on society disproportionate to their numbers, the debate over whether or not Shakespeare should be read by college freshmen is far less relevant to higher education today than the debate over how to teach college freshmen how to read. The experiences of the people in this book suggest that too much attention has been devoted to issues that are ultimately of marginal importance to the rank and file of most students and most professors. That does not mean the curriculum is unimportant, only that other forces play a more significant role in shaping higher education.

The changes in higher education are not confined to the humanities. In fact, subjects like history and literature comprise a small and rapidly shrinking proportion of the curriculum, and fewer students major in these subjects than ever before. The expansion of university athletic programs, especially at state schools, has dramatically altered student life and fund-raising. The proliferation of preprofessional schools, from law to nursing, from hotel management to public health, means that the undergraduate college must compete for resources and attention at most universities. Science programs continue to adjust to the influx of hundreds of billions of dollars in federal research money during the cold war and the contraction of that money today. Questions about affirmative action, the rights of disabled students, and student aid divide many campuses and generate enmity among students, parents, administrators, and politicians.

These and other issues have been largely absent from the preceding pages. A complete picture of higher education would include these elements, but the central issues discussed here would not therefore recede in importance. If anything, the guild orientation of the professoriate has as many negative ramifications on college athletics, affirmative action, and science funding as it does for humanities education, national identity, graduate school, and academic labor. The same impulses that keep professors detached from their students, from society, and from each other also keep them from addressing the university as a whole unit. The same attitudes that orient professors to the guild above all else keep them from applying their energies to redefining the university as a whole in the next millennium.

The mold of the research scholar is far too narrow to encompass the many tasks that professors are now called on to perform. One solution, of course, is to destroy the mold and make a new one. End tenure, cease to emphasize research, and begin the long process of redefinition. But this would be a great loss, and an unnecessary one. In the case of higher education today, it is possible for professors, students, parents, and the society as a whole to have their cake and eat it too.

That might come as a surprise to many professors, who defend tenure as an absolute good and who uphold the ideal of the research scholar against what they see as a capital-rich and idea-poor society. When faced with various alternatives, professors often reduce discussions of change to an "either/or" argument: "Either absolute tenure and protected academic freedom, or no tenure and no freedom." "Either train graduate students to be scholars, or there will be no research." "Either define scholarship as the primary purpose of professors, or knowledge will not be advanced and preserved." "Either resist the efforts of students, administrators, and legislators to determine what goes on in the classroom, or say good-bye to intellectual rigor and difficult ideas."

Faced with problems such as adjuncting and classroom struggles with students, professors tend to blame everyone but themselves. Some lament that students today aren't as disciplined, that they don't seem to care about learning as much as they care about securing their future. How can subjects like history and literature survive if students believe that anything unrelated to their economic future is frivolous? Professors and graduate students spend an inordinate amount of time at professional gatherings complaining about student apathy, implying that if only students were like them, the classroom would be more vibrant and the country better educated.

Others excoriate the culture at large. "It's not that a left-wing professorial coup has taken over the university," writes University of Virginia professor Mark Edmundson. "It's that at American universities left-liberal politics have collided with the ethos of consumerism. The consumer ethos is winning."[1] Entering the university with the attitude of consumers, students grade their classes and their professors on student evaluations much as *Consumer Reports* rates dishwashers. Deans and administrators, competing for students in a competitive market, respond to student and parental whims, and educational standards are the casualty.

Still others observe the plight of graduate students and adjuncts and respond with a resigned shrug. "What can we do?" Faculty at elite private schools shudder and perhaps reflect briefly that there but for the grace of God go I. But professors at Stanford and Williams College are as removed from underemployed adjuncts as they are from the urban homeless. They might feel guilty that we live in a society that contains such injustices, but they don't necessarily see the economy of higher education as their problem.

And of course, some professors point to conservative critics and legislators as the culprits for whatever tensions exist in the university. For these professors, we live in a society permeated by anti-intellectualism, and today's unfettered capitalism provides fertile ground for an attack on anything that doesn't directly generate income. Thank God for tenure, or else the barbarians would storm through the gates.

Professors are right to say that they shouldn't shoulder the blame for the tugs-of-war over the university and the humanities. But it is not true that nothing can be done. In fact, vast changes are occurring, and higher education is being redefined by community colleges, part-time and mature students, new schools, and expanding enrollments. This redefinition is chaotic, disorganized, and it's taking place without much input from those who still retain the most powerful voice in university governance: the professors themselves.

In short, if professors do not begin to respond, and respond actively, to the changes that are occurring, higher education will be redefined without them or in spite of them. If that happens, if professors remain passive resistors of change or active opponents of innovation, then much of what they fear may in fact come to pass. If they oppose the genuine efforts of state legislators to balance low tuition and universal access against tenure and scholarship, then they will be seen as bastions of an old guard that needs to be swept away. If they reject attempts to broaden the spectrum of what constitutes "professional work," then students, politicians, and society as a whole will view scholarship as an unaffordable luxury and a pernicious impediment to teaching and service. And if they resist the efforts of the other owners of the university to define what goes on in the university, they will ultimately be pushed to the margins because in the end, these other owners pay their salaries.

Professors are not solely responsible for the shape of higher education, but they are the only element in the equation that is cohesive enough to change. Academic guilds at present are controlled by a small number of professors at a small number of schools. Either these guilds need to expand their definition of academia, or the hundreds of thousands of professors and graduate students who work outside of the top research universities will expand it for them.

Two factors are at work. One is the demographic shift of the past two decades; the other is the economic chasm that has developed between the haves and have-nots of academe. The rapid growth of the community college system and public universities means that the need for research scholars is proportionately lower than it ever has been. The economic chasm shows that the model of the research scholar is not just anachronistic but destructive when applied too broadly.

What is to be done? Society needs these research scholars. We need people who will keep alive knowledge of the elegiac poets, who will flesh out life in rural New Hampshire on the eve of the revolution, who will preserve folk art of the nineteenth century, and who will illuminate the worlds of James Fenimore Cooper and Walt Whitman.[2] These scholars are a key component of our collective self-knowledge and therefore vital to the health of our society.

But this function can be fulfilled by hundreds of scholars in each discipline and subdiscipline working at fifty, a hundred, or even as many as two hundred colleges and universities. Other countries are able to maintain their "mystic chords of memory" with far fewer elite institutions of higher learning, and even compensating for the size and sophistication of the United States, it is hard to argue that more is necessary.

In fact, surveying the terrain of higher education in the United States, it seems that more may be less. More schools try to establish themselves as research centers in order to enhance their reputation, raise private money, and draw the best faculty. Faculty then devote their energies to research, duplicating and triplicating the work of their colleagues at the established research schools. As many academics are now realizing, more and more is written about less and less. Academic journals proliferate, but the readership does not. Schools spend money and sacrifice teaching time in order to give professors the opportunity to produce research, but as Berkeley's John

Searle commented, "Is it really necessary to have seventy-five books on the early poems of John Donne?"[3]

In the forest of contemporary academic research, the purpose of scholarship and the purpose of the university get lost. Research is conducted because the guild requires it, irrespective of whether society needs it ad infinitum. For many graduate students and professors, the purpose of the university is to provide them with books, office space, money, and time in order to do that research. The guilds have come to enshrine professionalism for its own sake, and in the process they are jeopardizing both the integrity of scholarship and the needs of the larger society.

For decades to come, several dozen major private universities will be able to preserve the model of the research scholar and train new generations of graduate students. Provided that stock and bond markets do not utterly collapse, places such as the Ivy League schools, the University of Chicago, Stanford, Georgetown, Washington University, Vanderbilt, and MIT will have billions in endowment money that will permit them to fund research and the necessary infrastructure.[4] A handful of private colleges will be able to promote an eclectic mix of scholarship and small classes. And dozens of public universities, with a mix of public funds and endowment income, will act for all intents and purposes like the Ivies.

And as for the rest? As for the other 3,000 colleges and universities? Here, in the new world of higher education, the research scholar needs to give way to the public servant-teacher. In terms of academic guilds, that is a radical notion. In terms of society's needs, it is imperative.

Looking at the professional organizations, listening to professors and graduate students, and assessing what is being said, I found little indication that the necessary changes will come from the center. At most, groups like the Modern Language Association, the American Historical Association, and the American Association of University Professors address the problems rhetorically. The various leaders of these groups will issue a statement, form a committee, and lament their inability to do anything about social forces beyond their control.

These organizations may not be able to redefine higher education single-handedly, but they certainly try to maintain a definition of the university that excludes more than it includes. At present, they aggravate and intensify the confusion surrounding the role of higher education and the humanities in American society, and they often impede the efforts of individual professors, students, and schools to innovate. The guilds may never be a source of experimentation. They could, however, make such experimentation much easier.

In the case of tenure reform, the guilds stigmatize any attempts to reconceptualize academic employment. Tenure is perfectly justifiable at a school that can afford it, but it is a travesty when the money for tenure doesn't exist. In the community colleges, defending tenure is tantamount to homeless people refusing low-income housing because they can only envision themselves in a mansion. It would be lovely to live in that mansion, but the all-or-nothing approach guarantees that the underemployed in academia will remain underemployed and exploited. Granted, the guilds could also think of ways to detach tenure from its current salary scale. Professors could have assured employment, but not necessarily assured income at the current level that tenure commands.

It's probably true that guilds by their very nature don't possess the capacity for radical change. They exist to uphold the norms, define the profession, and maintain standards and continuity. It would be nice to think that at the next meeting of the Modern Language Association, the powers-that-be will take the same hard look at academic employment and the model of the research scholar that they do at Jane Austen and "transgressive fiction." It would be wonderful if the chairpersons of the AAUP examine the costs and benefits of adjuncting with the same analytical rigor that they demand of their graduate students.

That's not going to happen. Prescriptions for change that urge these organizations to consider the unthinkable won't work, because they will be absorbed by these institutions as words without action. The same might be said of Congress, or various bureaucracies in Washington. Committees are formed; panels convened; documents gathered; reports written; nothing changes.

However, it seems within the realm of possibility to call on these organizations, and the professors who compose them, to stop obstructing change. Professional organizations, with their membership dues, lobbyists, and access to the media, effectively curtail creative solutions to academic underemployment, and they discourage alternate visions of academic work. Structurally, they are governed by and perpetuate a hierarchy that places the research scholar at the top of a steep pyramid, and they have a vested interest in maintaining the current status quo. But they could simultaneously defend absolute tenure along with scholarly research and embrace new paradigms. They could encourage multiple approaches to higher education without renouncing the particular one they hold dear.

Whether or not the guilds facilitate or obstruct the evolution of universal higher education, demographics are creating major shifts. In response to a flood of enrollments that may increase by more than 20 percent in the coming decades,[5] community colleges, new state campuses, and less-well-known private schools are exploring ways to reconceive higher education. Professors are hired on multiyear contracts rather than tenure; graduate students are trained as teachers rather than scholars; professors are encouraged to work with community organizations, both public and private, to address the needs of the surrounding environment; teaching loads are increased, while research expectations are lowered.

These experiments may be inimical to the research scholar, but they are beneficial to students and to the larger society. They also enrich the school, sometimes literally. Encouraging an English professor to assist local school boards in designing high school curricula doesn't just connect the university to the community. It may also enhance the salary of the professor, and perhaps the income of the department. Allowing an African American assistant professor to work with city hall in addressing issues of race relations in lieu of teaching an extra course not only makes academia relevant, but it satisfies the need of the larger society to have informed voices contributing to public debate.

Of course, professors, even when fulfilling these functions, don't necessarily do a good job. Professors are as capable of severe misjudgment and biases as the rest of us, and their solutions to complex social problems are just as apt to go awry. Their human failings hardly disqualify them from the opportunity to participate in the society around them. The expectations of the guild do.

If the stories told in these pages suggest anything, it is that the grip of the guilds must be loosened. These guilds color every aspect of higher education today, and aside from those hundred or so select institutions, the effect is deleterious. The guilds are more than the specific professional organizations; they encompass the majority of professors and graduate students. Professors often speak of "a community of scholars," with all the connotations of blood and belonging. Once, perhaps, these communities provided comfort and encouragement to the lonely few who undertook a life of research on the islands of higher education. In the nineteenth and early twentieth centuries, academia was a marginal force in American society. Professors needed that community of scholars, because without it, they were truly alone and largely ignored. This cozy, often petty, often stimulating community can no more serve the needs of contemporary higher education than a two-lane country road can meet the demands of a modern urban commute. As members of this community, professors resemble the aristocrats of 1780s France, unable and unwilling to respond to the sea changes taking place in front of their eyes.

Though the guilds must relax their definition of what constitutes professional work, that is much easier said than done.

The guilds are made up of individuals, and many individual professors have so internalized the norms of the profession that changes of the nature described in this book are inconceivable. Some believe that the center must hold, or civilization will be imperiled. Others are less hyperbolic, and defend the status quo in reasoned tones and gentle admonitions to those who would overturn it. The professorial rank and file are too busy with securing their future to think much about big pictures, and graduate students are caught between their idealism that things could be different and their cynicism that things will inevitably take a turn for the worse.

These individuals, like the guilds of which they are a part, are being overwhelmed by the expansion of higher education. Accompanying any growth of this magnitude is dislocation, but as the economist Joseph Schumpeter observed about capitalism, developments follow a pattern of creative destruction. As the old order decays and breaks up, new alternatives and new models proliferate. There are signs that this is happening in American higher education today. While only a handful of schools have undertaken meaningful tenure reform, an increasing number of people are questioning the absolutism that surrounds discussions of tenure. Many graduate students embrace the guild, but as the crisis in academic employment shows no signs of abating, others are starting to rebel against an often exploitative system. It is also becoming increasingly difficult to ignore the plight of the adjuncts.

Some schools have explicitly replaced the emphasis on research with an emphasis on teaching. It will take years of trial and error before academics can effectively measure good teaching and distinguish it from poor teaching. Student evaluations are a useful guide, but the consumer ethos of today's students often interferes with a sober assessment. Education schools have their own theories about what constitutes effective teaching, but like many students, education specialists prefer to focus on the process of learning rather than on content. In any event, teaching evaluation is still in its infancy, especially compared to a centuries-old tradition of judging scholarship. Professors are trained to judge scholarship, but they are only beginning to learn about teaching.

The most effective way to widen the scope of the profession is to encourage local variety. From the vantage point of the guilds, that encouragement would consist of leaving innovative schools and professors alone and letting them innovate, whether it be tenure, curriculum, or community service. It's not that the guilds have the power to coerce errant schools, but expressions of displeasure, reproachful words, and a variety of factors that combine to hurt the reputation of a school within the profession are remarkably effective deterrents. In the high society of Edith Wharton, reputations and careers rose and fell on subtle words, raised eyebrows, and stolen glances. It doesn't take much in higher education today to poison the image of a school.

Individual professors can help by rewarding innovation in graduate school and among assistant professors. As long as only tenured professors are permitted to branch out as their passions dictate, only tenured professors will be free to innovate. As we have seen, it is a rare academic in today's environment who is tenured, and it is a rare tenured academic who emerges from fifteen years of serfdom with an agenda different from that of the guild that has made his career. Leaving innovation to the tenured comes close to being an oxymoron.

Unless a wider range of work is rewarded earlier, higher education will continue to generate faculty incapable of responding appropriately to the demands of contemporary society. The balance of power in the classroom will shift even more toward the consumer-student, and hundreds of billions of dollars will continue to be spent for credentials alone. So much more is possible.

As higher education continues to democratize, it may lose some of what makes it distinct from the larger society. But for the most part, those places that can afford to remain separate will continue to do so, while those that cannot never fit the idyll of quiet quads in the first place. Making more scholarship and academic research relevant doesn't mean that all scholarship should be relevant. Some schools will continue to offer refuge from the market, and some professors will be paid to do work whose audience is limited and whose importance is not always apparent. Expanding the definition of academic work, therefore, does not require sacrifice. Quite the contrary. The current definition demands too high a price for students, professors, parents, and society.

As for the larger society, it would help if we focused less on making sure that everyone gets a college degree and more on what that college degree consists of. What is it about college that is supposed to give Americans an edge in the marketplace? What skills do we think college provides that allow an individual to thrive in the material world? And is contemporary higher education providing those skills? The stories in this book don't offer a clear answer to these questions, but they do point to a lack of serious discussion about them. Like health care, defense, social security, and campaign finance, higher education is now an issue that affects all of us. I have offered one perspective about the future of this public institution; there are others, many of which point in different directions. No one model, no simple answer, no overarching reform can possibly meet the needs of a system that encompasses 3,500 separate schools, millions of teachers, tens of millions of students, and billions of dollars. The strength of American higher education is its variety, and any attempts to homogenize the experience not only are bound to fail but also undermine the system's strengths.

So let the university be a place with multiple owners, each with their own vision. Let each have a voice in preserving, constructing, and developing the American college. The result may not be neat; it may be unwieldy. But it will serve an American society that has since the beginning been messy, contradictory, and at its best, incredibly vibrant and astonishingly creative.

NOTES

INTRODUCTION

1. In the summer of 1997, Congress passed the Taxpayer Relief Act, which took effect in January 1998. See Douglas Lederman, "The Politicking and Policy Making Behind a $40-Billion Windfall," *Chronicle of Higher Education* (November 28, 1997), pp. A28-A32.

2. In April 1998, the Carnegie Endowment for the Advancement of Teaching released an extensive report documenting the widespread prevalence of those attitudes. See Robin Wilson, "Report Blasts Research Unessential for Poor Teaching of Undergraduates," *Chronicle of Higher Education* (April 24, 1998), p. A12. Many of the interviews I conducted, some of which are discussed in the pages of this book, support Carnegie's conclusions.

3. Figures are from *The Chronicle of Higher Education – Almanac* (1996); National Center for Education Statistics, "The Condition of Education 1997," website address http://nces.ed.gov. Statistics also taken from Christopher Lucas, *Crisis in the Academy: Rethinking Higher Education in America* (New York, 1996), pp. 12–25; Alvin Kernan, ed., *What's Happened to the Humanities* (Princeton, NJ, 1997), pp. 4, 18ff; Louis Menand, "Everybody Else's College Education," *New York Times Magazine* (April 20, 1997). There is some disparity in the numbers, depending on the source, most notably over the percentage of high school students who go

on to earn college degrees, ranging from a low of about 41 percent to a high of nearly 60 percent.

4. The current debate began with Allan Bloom, *The Closing of the American Mind* (New York, 1987) and continued with Dinesh D'Souza, *Illiberal Education: The Politics of Race and Sex on Campus* (New York, 1991). The response from the left can be sampled in Lawrence Levine, *The Opening of the American Mind* (Boston, 1996), and Gary Nash, Charlotte Crabtree, and Ross Dunn, *History on Trial: Culture Wars and the Teaching of the Past* (New York, 1997).

5. Stephen Joel Trachtenberg, "Preparing for Baby Boomers: Older Students Will Bring New Opportunities to Colleges," *Chronicle of Higher Education* (March 21, 1997).

6. See Elliott A. Krause, *The Death of the Guilds: Professions, States, and the Advance of Capitalism, 1930 to the Present* (New Haven, CN, 1997).

7. For a defense of academic jargon, see Michael Bérubé, *The Chronicle of Higher Education*, February 21, 1997.

8. Kathi Kern gave this talk at the American Historical Association conference in Atlanta at the AHA Annual Meeting in January 1996. In addition, she published a version of her talk in *Perspectives*, the newsletter of the AHA (Kathi Kern, "To Feel a Part of History: Rethinking the U.S. History Survey," *Perspectives*, May/June 1996). The account here is based on my notes from the talk, though I have also drawn from the printed version. The latter, however, left out some of the more discursive, informal aspects of the talk.

CHAPTER ONE

1. *The Battalion* (October 24, 1996).

2. Crey Goldberg, "A Drinking Death Rattles Elite M.I.T.," *New York Times* (October 1, 1997), p. A12.

3. Richard Chacon, "Debt Burden Soaring for U.S. Students," *Boston Globe* (October 23, 1997); Carol Marie Cooper, "Dropping the Ball in Juggling Loans," *New York Times* (October 1, 1997), p. D1; Stephen Burd, "Community Colleges Seek Right to Limit Borrowing by Students," *Chronicle of Higher Education* (October 17, 1997), p. A35. Work figures are from "The Condition of Education 1997, Indicator 13," National Center for Education Statistics Website, op. cit.

4. There is a lively debate on whether or not a college education is as important in getting a good job as most people think. Marc Levinson, "Hire Education," *Newsweek* (September 30, 1996). The survey results were reported in "College Freshmen Aiming for High Marks in Income," *New York Times* (January 12, 1998), p. A14.

5. Peter Schmidt, "West Virginia Starts Sweeping Overhaul of Public Higher Education," *Chronicle of Higher Education* (July 26, 1996), p. A28.

6. James Ledbetter, "Bad News: The Slow, Sad Sellout of Journalism School"; Bryan Urstadt, "Get Rich-Quick Professor"; Stephen Glass, "The College Rankings Scam," *Rolling Stone* (October 16, 1997).

7. "Rip-Off! Inside the Higher Education Racket and 7 Ways You Can Make College More Affordable," *Boston Magazine* (November 1997).

8. These comments come from posting to WMST-L@ UMDD.UMD.EDU (Women's Studies List), a moderated group operated by H-Net: Humanities On-Line. Other groups include H-AMSTDY@MSU.EDU (American Studies), H-TEACH@ H-NET.MSU.EDU (Teaching), and H-SURVEY@H NET.MSU.EDU (Teaching the U.S. History Survey). There are a number of books that survey student life, including: Paul Rogat Loeb, *Generation at the Crossroads: Apathy and Action on the American Campus* (New

Brunswick, NJ, 1994); Kevin Coyne, *Domers: A Year at Notre Dame* (New York, 1995); P.F. Kluge, *Alma Mater: A College Homecoming* (Reading, MA, 1993); Jane Tompkins, *A Life in School: What the Teacher Learned* (Reading, MA, 1996); Peter Sacks, *Generation X Goes to College* (Chicago, 1996); Anne Matthews, *Bright College Years* (New York, 1997).

9. For a scathing indictment of rising college costs, see Erik Larson, "Why Colleges Cost Too Much," *Time/CNN Special Investigation* (March 1997); also, Tom Morganthau and Seema Nayyar, "Those Scary College Costs," *Newsweek* (April 29, 1996).

10. "College Tuition Rates Show Steady Growth, Report Says," *New York Times* (September 26, 1996).

11. Many people argue that any tax subsidy of student loans will be a green light for universities and colleges to raise tuition. "Clinton Tax Break Plan Is Called a Tuition Prod," *New York Times* (February 10, 1997). A consistent critic of contemporary higher education, Chester Finn, excoriates President Clinton's tax-break plan; Chester Finn, "C For Effort," *National Review* (April 7, 1997). Others laud the plan as opening higher education to anyone, regardless of ability to pay. See statement of Lawrence Denardis, President, University of New Haven, before the House Ways and Means Committee, March 5, 1997.

12. For a particularly glaring example of the student consumer mentality, and the degree to which it is even encouraged by colleges, see Myles Brand (president of Indiana University), "Universities Make Students Their Customers," *Indiana Daily Student* (November 21, 1996).

13. Heather May, "Ex-Students Sue University Over Quality of Education," *Chronicle of Higher Education* (August 16, 1996), pp. A29–30.

14. Stories are legion on the moderated newsgroups. Also see Sacks, *Generation X Goes to College*; Daphne Patai and Noretta Koertge, *Professing Feminism: Cautionary Tales From the Strange World of Women's Studies* (New York, 1994); Gretchen von Loewe Kreuter, *Forgotten Promise: Race and Gender Wars on a Small College Campus* (New York, 1996).

15. John Yemma, "No Sale at Villanova: Cliffs Notes Take a Dive for Literature," *Boston Globe* (April 19, 1997), p. A6.

16. Student comments from the spring of 1994 and the summer of 1995. I am grateful to Ron Choy of the American Cultures department at UC-Berkeley for providing me with these and hundreds of others.

17. On Binghamton, see Bruce Clark, "The Next Move Is Mine," *Financial Times* (December 6/7, 1997).

18. Dinesh D'Souza, *Illiberal Education: The Politics of Race and Sex on Campus* (New York, 1991), pp. 24ff. Similar critiques are made by Richard Bernstein, *Dictatorship of Virtue: How the Battle Over Multiculturalism Is Reshaping Our Schools, Our Country, Our Lives* (New York, 1994); William Bennett, *The De-Valuing of America* (New York, 1992). For rebuttals of D'Souza and other critics, see Lawrence Levine, *The Opening of the American Mind* (Boston, 1996); Alice Jardine, "Illiberal Reporting," in Christopher Newfield and Ronald Strickland, eds., *After Political Correctness: The Humanities and Society in the 1990s* (Boulder, CO, 1995), pp. 128–37; Paul Lauter, "Political Correctness and the Attack on American Colleges," in Michael Bérubé and Cary Nelson, *Higher Education Under Fire: Politics, Economics, and the Crisis of the Humanities* (New York, 1995), pp. 73–90; John K. Wilson, *The Myth of Political Correctness: The Conservative Attack on Higher Education* (Durham, NC, 1995), pp. 64–89; Lillian Robinson, *In the*

Canon's Mouth: Dispatches from the Culture Wars (Bloomington, IN, 1997).

19. One of the better philosophical defenses of the humanities can be found in Martha Nussbaum, *Cultivating Humanity: A Classical Defense of Reform in Liberal Education* (Cambridge, MA, 1997).

20. Lucia Perillo, "When the Classroom Becomes a Confessional," *Chronicle of Higher Education* (November 28, 1997), p. A56.

CHAPTER TWO

1. Data from *The Diversity Project: Final Report* (UC-Berkeley: Institute for the Study of Social Change, 1991 and 1995), p. iii.

2. Material provided by the Center for the Teaching and Study of American Culture, Wheeler Hall, UC-Berkeley.

3. See, for example, Paolo Freire, *The Pedagogy of the Oppressed* (New York, 1970). Freire applies Foucault's notions of power and hegemony to educational structures.

CHAPTER THREE

1. This figure includes doctors of education as well. See tables and figures on B.A.'s and Ph.D.'s in the appendix to *What's Happened to the Humanities*, op. cit. The figures are compiled from data provided by the National Center for Education Statistics.

2. William G. Bowen and Neil L. Rudenstine, *In Pursuit of the Ph.D.* (Princeton, NJ, 1992), pp. 56ff. Also, Kernan, *What's Happened to the Humanities*, pp. 252–53. There are actually fewer Ph.D.'s in humanities fields such as history and English than there were in the early 1970s. From a high of 5,200 humanities Ph.D.'s

in 1973, the number hovered around 4,000 per year in the mid-1990s.

3. Robert Townsend, "Studies Report Mixed News for History Job Seekers," *AHA Perspectives* (March 1997), pp. 7–10; Louis Menand, "How to Make the Ph.D. Matter," *New York Times Magazine* (September 22, 1996), p. 78.

4. For excellent studies of the unchanging culture of graduate education, see David Damrosch, *We Scholars* (Cambridge, MA, 1995); Alan Wolfe, "The Feudal Culture of the Postmodern University," *The Wilson Quarterly* (Winter 1996), pp. 54–66.

5. Bruce Kuklick, "The Emergence of the Humanities," in Darryl J. Gless and Barbara Hernstein Smith, eds., *The Politics of Liberal Education* (Durham, NC, 1992), pp. 201–12. For the debt to German academia, see Peter Novick, *That Noble Dream: The "Objectivity Question" and the American Historical Profession* (New York, 1988), pp. 21–108.

6. For wonderful descriptions of these worlds, see William Manchester, *A World Lit Only by Fire: The Medieval Mind and the Renaissance* (Boston, 1992). Also, L. D. Reynolds and N. G. Wilson, *Scribes & Scholars: A Guide to the Transmission of Greek and Latin Literature* (Oxford, 1974).

7. For the evolution of the professional academic organization, see Julie Reuben, *The Making of the Modern University* (Chicago, 1996), pp. 143ff; Gerald Graff, *Professing Literature: An Institutional History* (Chicago, 1987), pp. 19–98.

8. Excerpt from the mission statement of the American Association of University Professors, available on the Web page of the AAUP, http://www.igc.apc.org/aaup.

9. The dependency of graduate students on their mentors can take ugly turns when students feel betrayed. On rare but consistent occasions, graduate students physically assault or even kill their ad-

visors if they feel that their professors haven't lived up to their end of the bargain. See Courtney Leatherman, "Relations Between Graduate Students and Their Mentors, Though Rarely Violent, Are Often Fraught with Tension," *Chronicle of Higher Education* (September 6, 1996), pp. A15–16.

10. Marye Anne Fox, "Graduate Students: Too Many and Too Narrow?" in Ronald Ehrenberg, ed., *The American University: National Treasures or Endangered Species* (Ithaca, NY, 1997), pp. 100–114.

11. Christopher Wolff (Dean of the Graduate School of Arts and Sciences), "Brighter Forecasts Than We've Seen in Years," *Harvard Graduate School Alumni Association Newsletter* (Winter 1996).

12. Christina Boufis and Victoria C. Olsen, *On the Market: Surviving the Academic Job Search* (New York, 1997).

13. Jordan Ellenberg, "The Great Ph.D. Scam," *The Boston Phoenix* (March 7, 1997), p. 5.

14. Robert Townsend, "AHA Surveys Indicate Bleak Outlook in History Job Market," *AHA Perspectives* (April 1997).

15. Harry Bowen and Jack Schuster, *American Professors: A National Resource Imperiled* (New York, 1986), pp. 176–77.

16. Townsend, op. cit.

17. James Surowiecki, "Learning to Cope," *Boston Phoenix* (March 7, 1997), p. 7.

18. Interview with author.

19. For a critique of the wall between graduate study and the larger society, see Louis Menand, "How to Make the Ph.D. Matter," *New York Times Magazine* (September 22, 1996), pp. 78–82.

20. George Judson, "A Lesson in Limbo: Inside the World of Graduate Teaching Assistants," *New York Times: Education Life* (March 31, 1996); Cary Nelson, *Manifesto of a Tenured Radical* (New York, 1997), pp. 137ff. The lack of teacher training is an old issue. See Jack Schuster, Daniel Wheeler, et al., *Enhancing Faculty Careers: Strategies for Development and Renewal* (San Francisco, 1990), pp. 70–80.

21. The strike received extensive national press coverage. For detailed accounts and explanations, see Barbara Ehrenreich, Andrew Ross, Cary Nelson, Michael Bérubé, et al., "A Yale Strike Dossier," *Social Text* (Issue 49), pp. 1–131; Nelson, *Manifesto*, pp. 194ff.

22. Peter Brooks, "Graduate Learning as Apprenticeship," *Chronicle of Higher Education* (December 20, 1996), p. A52; Amy Wallace, "Teaching Assistants Call Strike at UCLA," *Los Angeles Times* (November 18, 1996); Matea Gold, "Response Mixed on UCLA Teaching Assistant Strike," *Los Angeles Times* (November 19, 1996); Bryce Baer, "UC Graduate Students Push for Collective Bargaining Rights," *Daily News—University of California, Santa Barbara* (November 19, 1996). For an overview of graduate student unionization efforts, see Courtney Leatherman, "As Teaching Assistants Push to Unionize, Debate Grows over What They Would Gain," *Chronicle of Higher Education* (October 3, 1997), p. A12.

23. Nelson, passim; *Social Text* (Issue 49). For a wider overview of faculty uneasiness with graduate-student organizing, see Courtney Leatherman and Denise Magner, "Faculty and Graduate-Student Strife over Job Issues Flares on Many Campuses," *Chronicle of Higher Education* (November 29, 1996), pp. A12–14.

24. This difficulty was explained in detail by Bowen and Rudenstine, op. cit.

25. Tom McIntyre, "You're Going to Teach Where?!" *Education Update* (September 1997).

26. Jules LaPidus, "Why Pursuing a Ph.D. Is a Risky Business," *Chronicle of Higher Education* (November 14, 1997), p. A60. Also see Donald Kennedy, former president of Stanford University, for a more nuanced but still rosy view of graduate education. Kennedy, *Academic Duty* (Cambridge, MA, 1997), pp. 22–58.

27. Robert Atwell, "Doctoral Education Must Match the Nation's Needs and the Realities of the Marketplace," *Chronicle of Higher Education* (November 29, 1996), p. B4.

CHAPTER FOUR

1. It is this approach to history that so disturbs people like Dinesh D'Souza and Allan Bloom. For examples of this perspective on the humanities, see D'Souza, *Illiberal Education*, op. cit.; Allan Bloom, *The Closing of the American Mind*, op. cit.; Charles Sykes, *Profscam* (New York, 1988); Richard Bernstein, *Dictatorship of Virtue: How the Battle over Multiculturalism Is Reshaping Our Schools, Our Country, Our Lives* (New York, 1994); Arthur Schlesinger, *The Disuniting of America: Reflections on a Multicultural Society* (New York, 1991); Roger Kimball, *Tenured Radicals: How Politics Has Corrupted Our Higher Education* (New York, 1990).

2. This definition comes from Patricia Meyer Sparks, ed., *Advocacy in the Classroom* (New York, 1996).

3. There is a probing series of essays on academic freedom in Louis Menand, ed., *The Future of Academic Freedom* (Princeton, NJ, 1996).

4. Chomsky has said this frequently throughout his career, most recently in *The Cold War and the University: Toward a New Intellectual History* (New York, 1997).

CHAPTER FIVE

1. Figures from William Honan, "University of Minnesota Regents Drop Effort to Modify Tenure," *New York Times* (November 17, 1996), p. 21; "Outlook for Higher Education in the 50 State Legislatures This Year," *Chronicle of Higher Education* (January 10, 1997), p. A36.

2. For an examination of spiraling costs at elite research universities, see Charles Clotfelter, *Buying the Best: Cost Escalation in Elite Higher Education* (Princeton, NJ, 1996).

3. "Time Line: 11 Months in Tenure's History," *Star Tribune* (November 1, 1996), p. 20A.

4. Introduction, *The Cold War and the University*, op. cit.

5. Donald Browne, "Tenure Brings Stability to the Whole University," *Star Tribune* (July 1, 1996), p. 11A.

6. Debra Eckerman Pitton, "Good Undergraduate Teaching Should Be a Higher Priority at 'U,'" *Star Tribune* (July 27, 1996), p. 21A.

7. Reagan's comments on NPR, *All Things Considered*, October 28, 1996.

8. This statement was widely publicized. One account can be found in a later article on the entire controversy. Rene Sanchez, "Minnesota Faculty, Regents Put Tenure to the Test," *Washington Post* (November 9, 1996), p. A1.

9. Comments of Professor Jim Tracy, *All Things Considered*, October 28, 1996.

10. Jim Dawson, "Will Keffeler's Departure End Stalemate?" *Star Tribune* (November 3, 1996), p. 1B.

11. William Honan, "University of Minnesota Regents Drop Effort to Modify Tenure," *New York Times* (November 17, 1996), p. 21; George Pinney and Mary Jane Smetanka, "Regents Likely to Drop 'U' Layoff Plan," *Star Tribune* (November 7, 1996), p. 1A.

12. Comments made during a forum on *The NewsHour with Jim Lehrer*, November 25, 1996.

13. Ibid.

14. Todd Ackerman, "Taking Aim at Tenure," *Houston Chronicle* (October 21, 1996), p. A1; A. Phillips Brooks, "Tenure, Academia's Inviolable Code, Becomes Legislative Target," *Austin American-Statesman* (July 8, 1996), p. A1.

15. Quoted by Todd Ackerman, *Houston Chronicle*, ibid.

16. The A&M regents began formulating plans in 1994. Initially, two of the regents wanted to abolish tenure completely. See Todd

Ackerman, "A&M's Tenure Turmoil Eases as Regents Change Stance," *Houston Chronicle* (March 5, 1994); Debbie Graves, "A&M Regents May Overhaul Tenure Process," *Austin American-Statesman* (March 5, 1994).

17. The primer on anti-intellectualism is Richard Hofstadter, *Anti-Intellectualism in American Life* (New York, 1963).

18. Mary Ann Roser, "UT Faculty Warned to Change Tenure," *Austin American-Statesman* (September 18, 1996), p. B1.

19. Mary Ann Roser, "Tenure at UT Is under Review," *Austin American-Statesman* (September 2, 1996), p. A1.

20. Bryan Mealer, "Faculty Asks Delay of Tenure Changes," *UT-Austin Daily Texan* (September 23, 1996).

21. Ibid.

22. Comments of Samuel Freeman quoted by Bryan Mealer, "UT Faculty Committee Attacks Tenure Policies," *UT-Austin Daily Texan* (September 27, 1996).

23. Mary Ann Roser, "Chancellor Proposes UT Faculty Peer Review," *Austin American-Statesman* (September 14, 1996), p. B1; and Roser, "Berdahl: Tenure Not in Peril at UT," *Austin American-Statesman* (September 17, 1996), p. B1.

24. Author interview with Boyd, October 1996.

25. Some professors, including self-professed liberals, have made this argument as well. Cary Nelson, "The Real Problem with Tenure Is Incompetent Faculty Hiring," *Chronicle of Higher Education* (November 14, 1997), pp. B4–5.

26. David Braybrooke, "Post-tenure Review System Would Harm Universities," *Austin American-Statesman* (October 10, 1996), p. A13.

27. Denise Magner, "U. of Texas, with an Eye on the Legislature, Starts a System of Post-Tenure Reviews," *Chronicle of Higher Education* (December 20, 1996), p. A10; Susan Jackson, "Joe Hill

Takes on Joe College," *Business Week* (December 23, 1996), p. 60; Mary Ann Roser, "Tenure Faces Biggest Test as Debate Spills Beyond Academe," *Austin American-Statesman* (November 10, 1996), p. A1.

28. Dennis Kelly, "New University Becomes Setting for Tenure Debate," *USA Today* (July 17, 1996), p. 6D. On escalating costs, see previous citations, as well as Peter Applebome, "Rising College Costs Imperil the Nation, Blunt Report Says," *New York Times* (June 18, 1996), p. A1.

29. Norman Draper, "Cloudy Horizons at the U," *Star Tribune* (December 9, 1996), p. 1A.

30. AAUP letter, February 14, 1997; ttp://www.igc.apc.org/aaup.

31. Denise Magner, "A Scholar Provides an Intellectual Framework for Plans to End or Revamp Tenure Systems," *Chronicle of Higher Education* (February 14, 1997), p. A10. Also, interview with author, April 1, 1997. For a brief articulation of Chait's views, see Chait, "Rethinking Tenure: Toward New Templates for Academic Employment," *Harvard Magazine* (July–August 1997), pp. 30–31.

32. For the most aggressive defense of tenure, see Matthew Finkin, *The Case for Tenure* (Ithaca, NY, 1996). Also, see Walter Metzger's excellent 1969 essay on the origins and rationale for tenure; Metzger, "Academic Freedom in Delocalized Academic Institutions," in Philip G. Altbach et al., eds., *Higher Education in American Society*, 3rd ed. (Amherst, NY, 1994), pp. 37–53.

33. For a reasoned defense of tenure by a general secretary of the AAUP, see Ernst Benjamin, "Some Implications of Tenure for the Profession and Society," *AHA Perspectives* (April 1997).

34. Statistics from National Center of Education Statistics Website, "The Condition of Education 1997, Indicator 60."

35. The absence of these skills is documented by James Traub in his study of open admissions at New York's City College. Traub, *City*

on a Hill: Testing the American Dream at City College (Reading, MA, 1994).

36. See Mark Schwehn, *Exiles from Eden: Religion and the Academic Vocation in America* (New York, 1993).

37. Examples of these attacks can be found in Martin Anderson, *Impostors at the Temple: American Intellectuals Are Destroying Our Universities and Cheating Our Students of Their Future* (New York, 1992); Charles Sykes, *Profscam*, op. cit. A more moderate critique can be found in Robert and Jon Solomon, *Up the University: Re-Creating Higher Education in America* (Reading, MA, 1993).

38. "New University Becomes Setting for Tenure Debate," *USA Today*, op. cit.

39. Robin Wilson, "Bennington, After Eliminating Tenure, Attracts New Faculty Members and Students," *Chronicle of Higher Education* (January 10, 1997), p. A10.

40. Of course, the University of Phoenix is not without its detractors, who have called it the McDonald's of higher education. See James Traub, "Drive-Thru U.," *The New Yorker* (October 20/27, 1997), pp. 114–23.

41. Arthur Raines writing in *The Washington Post* (December 3, 1996).

42. National Center of Education Statistics, Indicator 60, op. cit.

CHAPTER SIX

1. See Ellen Schrecker, *No Ivory Tower: McCarthyism and the Universities* (New York, 1986); John Patrick Diggins, *The Rise and Fall of the American Left* (New York, 1992).

2. For an examination of these "public intellectuals," see Russell Jacoby, *The Last Intellectuals: American Culture in the Age of Academe* (New York, 1987).

3. A recent memoir of these years is Roger Rosenblatt, *Coming Apart: A Memoir of the Harvard Wars of 1969* (Boston, 1997). Also, Terry Anderson, *The Movement and the Sixties* (New York, 1995).

4. Everett Carll Ladd and Seymour Martin Lipset, *The Divided Academy: Professors & Politics* (New York, 1975).

5. Rosen has written widely on the nature of public scholarship, as have others under the auspices of the Kettering Foundation. See, for example, the essays in David Brown, ed., *Higher Education Exchange* (The Kettering Foundation, 1996).

6. Lisa Mighetto, "Careers in Public History: Consulting Offers a Variety of Opportunities," *AHA Persepctives* (December 1995); James Lide, "War's Unexpected Cost: Public Historians and Environmental Research," *Perspectives* (April 1996).

7. For a nuanced critique of public scholarship, see Alan Wolfe, "The Promise and Flaws of Public Scholarship," *Chronicle of Higher Education* (January 10, 1997), p. B4.

8. Janny Scott, "Scholars Fear Star System May Undercut Their Mission," *New York Times* (December 20, 1997), p. 1; John Yemma, "Profs Juggle Campus, Limelight," *Boston Globe* (September 11, 1996); Scot Lehigh, "Universities Flunk Idea Test," *Boston Globe* (March 3, 1996), p. 69.

9. Loïc J. D. Wacquant, "The Self-Inflicted Irrelevance of American Academics," *Academe* (July–August 1996).

10. John J. Piderit, "Where Universities Have Gone Wrong," *Wall Street Journal* (July 30, 1996).

11. Joyce Appleby, Lynn Hunt, and Margaret Jacobs, *Telling the Truth About History* (New York, 1994); Gerald Graff, "The Charge That Research Is Narrow and Opaque Is Decades Out of Date," *Chronicle of Higher Education* (October 21, 1992); Graff, "The Scholar in Society," *Introduction to Scholarship in Modern Languages and Literature* (New York: MLA, 1992).

12. For the perspective of three noted university presidents, see Clark Kerr, *The Uses of the University*, 4th ed. (Cambridge, 1963, 1995); Derek Bok, *Higher Learning* (Cambridge, 1986); Bok, *Beyond the Ivory Tower: Social Responsibilities of the Modern University* (Cambridge, 1982); James O. Freedom, *Idealism and Liberal Education* (Ann Arbor, 1996).

CHAPTER SEVEN

1. Many of these warnings came from the Reagan administration. See National Commission on Excellence in Education, *A Nation at Risk: the Imperative for Educational Reform* (Washington D.C., 1983).

2. Quoted in Gary Nash, Charlotte Crabtree, and Ross Dunn, *History on Trial: Culture Wars and the Teaching of the Past* (New York, 1997), p. 149.

3. "Title I—National Education Goals," H.R. 1804–6. For related articles, see Mark Pitsch, "Political Stakes Attached to Opportunity Standards," *Education Week* (February 23, 1994); Pitsch, "With Students' Aid, Clinton Signs Goals 2000," *Education Week* (April 6, 1994).

4. "Application to the National Endowment for the Humanities, Division of Education Programs," submitted by Charlotte Crabtree, Director, National Center for History in the Schools, UCLA, March 18, 1991. Archives for the center are located at the UCLA Library (hereafter NCHS Archives).

5. National Center for History in the Schools, *National Standards for United States History* (Los Angeles, 1994).

6. National Council for History Standards, "Criteria for Standards," May 1, 1992, UCLA Library.

7. For these debates see Nash, Crabtree, and Dunn, *History on Trial*, chapter 7, op. cit. Also, Paul Gagnon, "Why Study History?" *The Atlantic Monthly* (November 1988). Letter of William McNeill to Charlotte Crabtree, May 8, 1992; letter of Louise Tilly, President of the AHA, to Charlotte Crabtree and Gary Nash, May 17, 1993: NCHS Archives, UCLA.

8. Letter of Jay Taggert, Utah State Office of Education, to National History Standards Project, April 23, 1992: NCHS Archives. Other letters from state education officials made similar criticisms and suggestions.

9. Memo from Betram Wyatt-Brown, OAH Representative to OAH Focus Group Members and to Gary Nash and Charlotte Crabtree of the NCHS, "Report on the June 10–12, 1993, Meeting of the National Council for History Standards in Washington." NCHS Archives, UCLA.

10. Finn's position is described in Nash et al., *History on Trial*, pp. 109–11, 152–66. The specific characterization comes from author's interview with Nash, November 25, 1996, Los Angeles.

11. Comments of Lynne Cheney on *Good Morning, America*, October 27, 1994.

12. Transcript of Rush Limbaugh show, October 28, 1994.

13. Charles Krauthammer, "History Hijacked," *Washington Post* (November 4, 1994).

14. John Leo, "The Hijacking of American History," *U.S. News & World Report* (November 14, 1994).

15. John Patrick Diggins, "Historical Blindness," *New York Times* (November 19, 1994).

16. Ruth Rosen, "The War to Control the Past," *Los Angeles Times* (November 24, 1994).

17. Carol Gluck, "Let the Debate Continue?" *New York Times* (November 19, 1994).

18. Editorial, "A Blueprint of History for American Students," *San Francisco Chronicle* (November 1997).

19. Arnita Jones, "Our Stake in the History Standards," *Chronicle of Higher Education* (January 6, 1995).

20. Lynne Cheney, "Kill My Old Agency, Please," *The Wall Street Journal* (January 24, 1995). For the link between the attack on standards and the attack on the NEH, see Jon Weiner, "History Lesson," *The New Republic* (January 2, 1995).

21. Gorton's comments and text of resolution, *Congressional Record* (January 18, 1995), S.1026ff.

22. John Leo, "History Standards Are Bunk," *U.S. News & World Report* (February 6, 1995).

23. Editorial, "Maligning the History Standards," *New York Times* (February 13, 1995); Frank Rich, "Cheney Dumbs Down," *New York Times* (February 26, 1995); Diane Ravitch, "Revise, but Don't Abandon, the History Standards," *Chronicle of Higher Education* (February 17, 1995); Theodore Rabb and Akira Iriye, "Teach Whose Humanities?" *Philadelphia Inquirer* (April 1, 1995).

24. Leff to Moseley-Braun, March 14, 1995. NCHS Archives, UCLA.

25. Schlesinger to Nash, March 4, 1995; Nash to Schlesinger, April 18, 1995. NCHS Archives, UCLA. Paul Gagnon penned a critical but serious appraisal of the standards: Gagnon, "Botched Standards," *Atlantic Monthly* (December 1995).

26. Arthur Schlesinger and Diane Ravitch, "The New, Improved History Standards," *Wall Street Journal* (April 3, 1996).

27. John Patrick Diggins, "History Standards Get It Wrong Again," *New York Times* (May 15, 1996). For a longer version of this argument, see Diggins, "The National History Standards," *American Scholar* (Autumn 1996).

28. This argument is developed by Todd Gitlin. See Gitlin, *The Twilight of Common Dreams: Why America Is Wracked by Culture Wars* (New York, 1995), pp. 189ff. This wasn't the first time this fissure was exposed, and it followed on the heels of a blowup over a Smithsonian exhibit about the winning of the West. See Edward Linenthal and Tom Englehart, *History Wars: The Enola Gay and Other Battles for the American Past* (New York, 1996).

29. James Davison Hunter, *Culture Wars: The Struggle to Define America* (New York, 1991).

30. Lyn Nell Hancock, "History Lessons," *Newsweek* (July 10, 1995).

31. On the question of ownership, see Sarah Hinley, Spencer Crew, and Gary Nash,"Who Owns History? History in the Museum and in the Classroom," *AHA Perspectives* (October 1996); Natalie Zemon Davis, "Who Owns History? History in the Profession," *Perspectives* (November 1996).

32. David Denby, *Great Books* (New York, 1996). Vendler's review of Denby appeared in *The New Republic* (October 7, 1996).

33. Nash et al., *History on Trial*, p. 275.

CHAPTER EIGHT

1. Gloria's remarks were posted to a Usenet newsgroup on the Internet: H-AMSTDY@MSU.EDU, April 16, 1997.

2. Figures are from the AAUP Home Page, http://www.igc.apcorg/aaup/pttime.htm. Also see John Roueche, Suanne Roueche, and Mark Milliron, *Strangers in Their Own Land: Part-time Faculty in American Community Colleges* (Washington D.C, 1995); Vincent Tirelli, "Adjuncts and More Adjuncts," *Social Text* 51 (Summer 1997), pp. 76–80.

3. Michael Shenefelt, "Pity the Serfs at Our Medieval Universities," *New York Times* (January 13, 1987).

4. John Roueche et al., *Strangers in Their Own land,* op. cit.

5. Posted to H-AMSTDY@MSU.EDU, April 19, 1997.

6. For a heartbreaking account of the "eyes glazing over" phenomenon, see Evelyn Edison, "The Historian at the Community College," *AHA Perspectives* (October 1996).

7. Courtney Leatherman, "Growing Use of Part-Time Professors Prompts Debate and Calls for Action," *Chronicle of Higher Education* (October 10, 1997), p. A14; Courtney Leatherman, "Do Accreditors Look the Other Way When Colleges Rely on Part-Timers?" *Chronicle of Higher Education* (November 7, 1997), p. A12.

8. "Faculty at the University of Minnesota Reject Board Revisions to Tenure Code; AAUP Finds Proposed Revisions Threat to Academic Freedom," AAUP Web Page, op. cit.

9. For a brilliant and disturbing look at CUNY's City College, see James Traub, *City on a Hill: Testing the American Dream at City College* (Reading, MA, 1994).

10. The survey was conducted by the Higher Education Research Institute at the University of California at Los Angeles, findings excerpted in Denise Magner, "Fewer Professors Believe Western Culture Should Be the Cornerstone of the College Curriculum," *Chronicle of Higher Education* (September 13, 1996).

11. Edgar Boone, "National Perspective of Community Colleges," *Community College Journal of Research and Practice* (Number 21, 1997).

CHAPTER NINE

1. Karla Haworth, "President Vows to Make Education His Top Priority," *Chronicle of Higher Education* (February 14, 1997). On

the 1997 budget agreement, see assorted articles in *New York Times* (July 29–30, 1997).

2. William Henry, *In Defense of Elitism* (New York, 1994); Nicholas Lehman, "The Rise of the Meritocracy," *Atlantic Monthly* (1996). Lehman is also working on a book about the meritocracy and the growth of standardized testing.

3. Herbert Kliebard, *The Struggle for the American Curriculum: 1893–1958* (New York, 1995).

4. For example, John Dewey, *Democracy and Education: An Introduction to the Philosophy of Education* (New York, 1916). Also, Alan Ryan, *John Dewey: High Tide of Liberalism* (New York, 1995).

5. Traub, *City on a Hill*, op. cit.; Clifford Levy, "Guiliani Demands Community Colleges Drop Remedial Help," *New York Times* (January 30, 1998), p. B1.

6. On the productivity of higher education relative to other sectors, see Derek Bok, *The State of the Nation* (Cambridge, MA, 1996).

7. Joseph Nye, Philip Zelikow, and David King, *Why Americans Don't Trust Government* (Cambridge, MA, 1997).

8. According to a Hart-Teeter survey conducted in February 1997, 56 percent of the public support federal and state college loan programs.

9. The Harris Poll (January 1997).

10. The most intense version of that critique is Robert Bork, *Slouching Towards Gomorrah* (New York, 1997). More moderate versions are cited earlier.

11. Robert Hughes bitingly dismisses what he calls the patriotic correctness of the right and the political correctness of the left: Hughes, *The Culture of Complaint* (New York, 1993).

12. Roger Kimball, "The Killing of History," *The New Criterion* (September 1996); Edith Kuzweil and William Phillips, eds., *Our*

Country, Our Culture: The Politics of Political Correctness (Boston, 1994); Gertrude Himmelfarb, *The New History and the Old* (Cambridge, MA, 1987); Russell Jacoby, *Dogmatic Wisdom* (New York, 1994); Lawrence Levine, *The Opening of the American Mind*, op. cit.; Joyce Appleby, Margaret Jacobs, Lynne Hunt, *Telling the Truth about History*, op. cit.; David Harlan, *The Degradation of American History* (Chicago, 1997).

13. Kay Hymowitz, "J. Crew U.," *City Journal* (Spring 1996).

14. James Perley and Mary Burgan, "Comments and Recommendations Submitted to the Office of Postsecondary Education, Department of Education, December 17, 1996," AAUP Web Page, op. cit.

15. Michael Marriott, "Taking Education Beyond the Classroom," and Gustav Niebuhr, "Colleges Setting Moral Compass," *New York Times Education Life* (August 4, 1996).

16. George Marsden, *The Soul of the American University* (New York, 1994).

17. Even some of the staunchest defenders of "the canon" have begun to realize this, albeit grudgingly. See Nathan Glazer, *We Are All Multiculturalists Now* (Cambridge, MA, 1997). For a superbly balanced look at multiculturalism, see David Hollinger, *Postethnic America: Beyond Multiculturalism* (New York, 1995).

18. Thomas Geoghegan, "Overeducated and Underpaid," *New York Times* (June 3, 1997).

19. Alisa Valdés, "Silber Says College Isn't for Everyone," *Boston Globe* (February 13, 1997).

CONCLUSION

1. Mark Edmundson, "On the Uses of a Liberal Education," *Harper's* (September 1997).

2. Two superb Pulitzer Prize–winning books in the 1990s did just that. See Alan Taylor, *William Cooper's Town* (New York, 1995); David Reynolds, *Walt Whitman's America* (New York, 1996).

3. Interview with author.

4. In fact, university endowments are at all-time highs. Julie Nicklin, "Bull Market Helped Endowments Earn Average of 17.2% in 1996," *Chronicle of Higher Education* (February 14, 1997), p. A34.

5. Editorial, *New York Times* (August 23, 1997).

ACKNOWLEDGMENTS

Over the course of researching this book, I spoke with hundreds of people, some casually and some in the course of formal interviews. In addition, dozens of professors and graduate students allowed me to sit in on their classes and talk with their students Though I cannot name them all here, I thank each of them for their time and insights. Whether or not they are quoted in the book, their views shaped mine, and I hope I have done justice to theirs.

During my visits to different schools, several people graciously hosted me and helped me navigate through their campuses. They also shared their ideas and helped me refine my arguments. So to Fred Logevall at UC-Santa Barbara, Thomas Knock at Southern Methodist University, Femi Vaughan at SUNY-Stonybrook, and H. W. Brands at Texas A&M, thank you. Also thanks to Ron Choy at the American Cultures program at UC-Berkeley and Don Palm at the University of Texas-Austin.

In addition, many friends, colleagues, and family members read parts or all of earlier drafts of the book. For their criticism and insights, I am grateful to Deena Balboa, Peter Berkowitz, Derek Bok, Douglas Brinkley, Richard Bulliet, David Denby, Tiffany Devitt, John Patrick Diggins, Jennifer Gonzales, Gerald Graff, Lucinda Jewell, Marion Just, Jo Karabell, David Karabell, Kathleen Kendall, Lewis Lapham, Martin Lee, Scott Manus, Louis Menand, Timothy Naftali, Jay

Rosen, and Alan Wolfe. And to Colby Devitt, who not only read but listened and shared.

This book was also influenced by conversations over the years with numerous colleagues, friends, and teachers, particularly Jonathan Rosenberg, Neal Rosendorf, Amy Gluck Adachi, Jiro Adachi, Austen Ivereigh, Susan Freiwald, Eric Olson, Ernest May, Bernard Bailyn, Alan Brinkley, Roy Mottahedeh, Roger Owen, Akira Iriye, John Coatsworth, Frederick Schauer, Joseph Nye, Samuel Huntington, Steve Schwartzberg, Gideon Rose, Byron Winn, Kathryn Slanski, Kimerer Lamothe, David King, Russell Jacoby, James Carroll, Marvin Kalb, Thomas Patterson, Nancy Palmer, John Searle, Eric Foner, and Jim Shenton.

I owe a debt to my agent, John Hawkins, who made sure that this book would not be lost in the midst of a particularly tumultuous time in the publishing world. I am grateful for the input of my editors as this book made its peregrinations through that world. Paul Golob and Tim Duggan believed in this project and gave me needed support and advice. Don Fehr completed the process and infused his own insight. His enthusiasm and encouragement have been invaluable. Caroline Sparrow at Basic took care of the many and frequent details shepherding the book to completion. Richard Fumosa took good care of the book as it was transformed from a manuscript into a finished product. And thanks also to Sabrina Bracco, Marian Brown, Arlene Kriv, Peggy Lawlis, and Matthew Goldberg for their work in marketing and publicity.

And above all, this book is dedicated to Susan Rabiner, without whom it would not and could not have been written.

INDEX